WALKING WITH GOD

Reflections on Life's Meaning

Adolfo Quezada

LIGUORI
PUBLICATIONS

One Liguori Drive
Liguori, Missouri 63057-9999
(314) 464-2500

DEDICATION
To Judy,
On my mind,
in my spirit.
A. Q.

Imprimi Potest:
William A. Nugent, C.SS.R.
Provincial, St. Louis Province
The Redemptorists

Imprimatur:
Monsignor Maurice F. Byrne
Vice Chancellor, Archdiocese of St. Louis

ISBN 0-89243-320-5
Library of Congress Catalog Card Number: 90-60305

Copyright © 1990, Adolfo Quezada
Printed in U.S.A.

Scripture selections are taken from the NEW AMERICAN BIBLE WITH REVISED NEW TESTAMENT, copyright © 1986, by the Confraternity of Christian Doctrine, Washington, DC 20017, and are used by permission of copyright owner. All rights reserved.

TABLE
OF CONTENTS

PREFACE

Spirituality becomes little more than sentimentality unless we integrate it into the reality of our daily living. This book bridges the gap between our psychological and spiritual selves. It takes the thoughts, emotions, and physical senses that we all hold in common and permeates them with the energy of the spirit which we all share.

Regardless of our religious bent, if we fail to apply what we believe to how we live, we remain less than we are capable of becoming. This book challenges us to examine the foundation of our faith, to consider the nature of our prayer, and to allow the power of God to do its work in us.

Walking With God looks openly at our basic humanness, including our simplicity, weakness, gentleness, and vulnerability that we must come to embrace. This book offers us a look at some of the myths about life by which we have chosen to live, and it gives us an understanding of the impact that our emotions have on our daily living. It calls for love of self and for a full and honest response to life.

The theme which runs through these pages is that we are born to love and be loved. To love God with our entire being, to love ourselves as we love our neighbor, and to live in accord with this love is the purpose and meaning of life.

ALONENESS

When quiet comes and solitude has its day, our true selves are manifested. Alone and still, we touch the deepest chambers of our souls. In that instant we turn our backs on the demands, obligations, and expectations hounding us to forsake our ideals. We begin to think our own thoughts, feel our own feelings, and experience the true sense of ourselves. We remove our masks and listen to the words that come from our hearts. We come to discover our true wants and our most basic needs.

Being grounded in ourselves is the highest state we can attain. It is from this foundation that we can build toward our full potential. Centering is the process by which we come to know our essential selves. It brings a sense of balance into our lives.

When we are alone, we are thrown back upon our inner resources from which we derive the strength and courage to set our own directions and make our own choices. No longer dependent on others, we revel in the revelations of self-discovery. As we gain more consciousness of ourselves, our choices and our freedom also expand. And this in turn gives us a renewed faith in ourselves and our capabilities. We rise to our potential because we have a solid belief in ourselves as worthy human beings.

This joy of freedom makes us dream new dreams. We may suffer the pain that comes from growth and cry the tears that follow loss. We may stumble — even fall — but we will rise and meet the challenge of being fully human, fully ourselves.

The truth will set you free.

(John 8:32)

ANGER

W	e all feel anger at times. This basic human emotion can be denied only at the expense of our mental health.

Anger's strong feeling of displeasure is a reaction to being hurt. It is a valuable piece in our emotional arsenal and is designed to help us break down barriers to holistic living.

For many of us anger is synonymous with danger, and we live our lives guarding against its expression by others and by ourselves. But repressed anger causes anxiety and stress, and peace is impossible under those conditions.

We block out anger because we have been taught from an early age that this was the way to get along with people. To act in anger was usually considered bad behavior. But when anger is not acted out as anger, the causes for it — problems, differences with others, irritations with situations, misunderstandings in communication, and so forth — cannot be resolved.

Anger that is not hidden can actually help bring about peace by identifying problems and bringing them into the light where they can be faced. Buried anger is also buried hurt. Together they comprise the unresolved resentment that destroys our peace.

We may be afraid of expressing anger because we think that we will end up having a nervous breakdown. Or we fear that we may hurt someone physically or emotionally if we express the anger within us. Actually the opposite is true. We are more apt to become emotionally sick if we repress our anger than if we express it appropriately. Also, we are more apt to hurt others by holding in our anger until it explodes than if we express it to them when it first arises and before it builds.

When anger is repressed, it stays and festers within us. It becomes a force that seeks to break out one way or another. Usually it escapes at least into our unconscious and produces much anxiety and stress.

Unexpressed anger — especially if it is turned inward — may result in such psychosomatic disturbances as headaches, muscular tension, destruction of gums and teeth through teeth-grinding, disturbances of hearing and vision, skin eruptions, cardiovascular disorders, fever and sweating, gastrointestinal disorders, ulcers, or high blood pressure.

Sometimes unexpressed anger shows up in our proneness toward accidents, especially car accidents. We also act out and repress our anger through the abuse of drugs, tobacco, and food. Even obesity can be the result of eating binges that are simply unconscious temper tantrums.

Because we have been taught that it is not right to be angry at others, we tend to turn anger in on ourselves. We presume it is safer and more saintly to be angry at ourselves than at someone else.

We are under the misconception that anger turned inward instead of outward prevents conflict. It doesn't. In fact, the conflict within us is far more devastating than any outward conflict would be because it is a struggle between the healthy and natural expression of emotion and its unhealthy repression. It is a conflict that produces division within ourselves, making us feel incomplete and depressed.

Depression dissipates our anger and has a numbing, dulling, anesthetic effect that deadens not only our feelings of anger but also all our feelings, including joy, sadness, excitement, caring, and desire for closeness.

We deal best with anger by expressing it. But even before we express it, we need to really feel its presence. Consciously feeling our anger is a degree of expressing it, even if only to ourselves.

It helps us, too, when we can pinpoint the source of our anger.

Somehow understanding its origin puts our anger in perspective, and we are able to handle it more responsibly.

When we know what prompts our anger, we can better prepare for its inception and, even more, its prevention. Of course, it is better to prevent — not repress — anger if we can, but we must expect that all of us will get angry at one time or another.

Rather than trying to prevent anger at all costs, it is more important to know when and how we become angry and to treat it as an acceptable and even valuable feeling.

Expressed anger can be the catalyst for change, and change can sometimes bring us closer to others.

Anger by itself does not disturb our peace. It is only when we deny it or block its expression that it becomes our enemy.

> **Envy and anger shorten one's life,**
> **worry brings on premature old age.**
> **(Sirach 30:24)**

ANXIETY

Anxiety. Even the word itself disturbs our peace and conjures up images of psychological pain and turmoil.

And well it should. Anxiety is one of the greatest destroyers of our mental and spiritual health. It is among the most painful of human emotions. Suffered over a prolonged period, anxiety can affect our bodies and lead to physical illnesses.

What is so devastating about anxiety is that it is basically caused by fear of the unknown. When we fear something, we know we can focus our thoughts and actions on it and overcome its threat. With anxiety, on the other hand, we do not know the enemy and, consequently, do not know how to meet its threat to us.

Once we know what we are anxious about, it ceases to be anxiety and turns into a fear with which we can deal directly. In fear we can make a choice to protect ourselves. As soon as we become conscious of the enemy, we can cope, we can adjust, we can prepare our defenses. It is the *unknown* enemy that prompts anxiety and leaves us defenseless and scattered.

In responding to a fear of the *known* we are able to call upon mental, emotional, and physical faculties to act appropriately. We may run away from the danger or stay and fight it. But anxiety immobilizes us. We feel trapped and without the ability to fight or flee. Instead of being able to call upon our effective human faculties, our perception becomes confused and our movement impaired.

Anxiety is our reaction to a danger we sense or to a value or circumstance which we identify with our existence. Because many of us derive our sense of existence from our interaction with others, anxiety sometimes comes from our fear of being left alone, isolated, or lonely.

When we orient ourselves in life according to someone or something and that frame of reference is threatened, anxiety sets in. The extreme form of this kind of fear is called psychosis — a mental disorder characterized by delusions or hallucinations.

The more anxious we become about losing ourselves through lack of orientation, the more consciousness of ourselves is dulled. Anxiety tends to disorient us even more and robs us of our sense of who we are and what we are doing. In short, it muddles the reality around us.

When our anxiety is acute, when it is disproportionate to the real danger, we may be experiencing neurotic anxiety. This chronic anxiety usually emanates from an unconscious conflict within us, and to deal with this we need professional help.

Anxiety has its beneficial side as well. It signals us that a conflict exists within ourselves. As long as there is a conflict going on between our sense of wholeness and the danger to it, we can work toward a constructive solution. If we find ourselves beyond anxiety, beyond the internal conflict, and in a sense of resignation and apathy, we have lost the battle and our existence is indeed on the brink of extinction. We must use anxiety constructively by identifying the threat to our existence and facing it directly.

Since anxiety is capable of destroying the consciousness of selves, the reverse is also true. The more aware we become of ourselves, the more our anxiety is dissipated. Our task in the face of anxiety is to become more conscious of ourselves and to tap our inner source of strength.

Have no anxiety at all.
(Philippians 4:6)

11

BIRTHING
OF
LOVE

We are pregnant with the seed of God, and it is we who shall give birth to the Child of Love in the world.

God pursued us from the beginning, and he did not give up until we looked his way. We, who were afraid to commit lest we limit our opportunities, finally walked slowly toward the extended hand of God.

As we came to know him in prayer, our passion for God's presence grew until we could no longer resist. Instead of just saying prayers, we began to listen. We discovered that his love for us was unconditional; and we freely chose to betroth ourselves to him.

Our commitment, manifested by our total abandonment and availability to God, evolved into our marriage to him. From this intimate communion, from this entrance into one another, the Child of Love was conceived.

Within us, the Child of God is nurtured and protected. Within us, the Child moves and quickens our spirit. Soon the Child of Love will be born to impact on the world around us.

The birth of Love comes with pain. To share with the world a part of us which has been ours alone, hidden and personal, is threatening. Yet, going out of ourselves is the essence of all love.

In the beginning we will be careful where we allow Love to play, lest it be violated by abuse. As Love grows in strength and wisdom, we will allow it to roam further. Risks will be taken and love will live and work in the world of vulnerability. There, exposed to the enemies of greed, insecurity, selfishness, vengeance, and apathy, Love will venture into life courageously. There it will be found smiling at a stranger, consoling a friend, caressing a child, or serving the needs of another.

Love will not always appear to act rationally or practically, but in the end it will make the most sense. Risking rejection, it will become stronger as it acknowledges its weakness, and it will increase in stature as it gives itself away.

Love will endure hardships, will grieve losses, and will forgive hurts, but it will also defend when attacked at its core.

Love will listen openly. It will be patient with the limitations of others.

Love will give the gift of freedom to all those it encounters and will challenge the world to live more generously.

Love will heal with its gentleness of spirit and will face life realistically. Love will hate hypocrisy and will speak out against injustices, even in the face of danger.

Love is our child and the Child of God. This Child will give unto the world and the world will know it not. But we will know it and the One from whom it came, and we will be with him again and bear his fruit.

We love because he [God] first loved us.
(1 John 4:19)

CELEBRATING THE MOMENT

The gift of life with all its joy and splendor is in the moment at hand. Now it is ours to relish and enjoy; now it is ours to cherish and to hold, but only for the moment.

If we could, we would capture for ourselves the glorious birth of this new day as its sunlight breaks over eastern mountains, full of hope and promise. Yet, we cannot hold it still in all its beauty, for then the day would never come.

If we could, we would stay in the peace of our morning prayer in which we feel so loved and nourished. We would remain in the arms of our God who holds us so securely. Yet, we cannot stay for long, for in life we must give what we receive, we must work when we have rested, and we must live what we have prayed.

If we could, we would hold fast to the presence of our loved ones. We are completed in their midst. What pleasure to be together, to share our lives, to laugh and play, to cry and pray. But we cannot hold them forever. We cannot stop time. Instead, we must love and be loved in the moment at hand as though there were no other.

The moment of unconditional love in which our children hug us with all their might, the time of ecstasy atop a mountain as we survey the world, the total intimacy between two persons that may last but one short while — all these moments belong not to us but to the ages. Ours is but to live them fully and enjoy them completely while we have them, for soon we will be asked to let them go.

The gifts of the moment will not be possessed. We may eat their fruit and drink their refreshment, but they are not to keep. It is only when we release the moment at hand that it can enter into eternity. Then our arms are free to embrace the moment that comes.

We find that we have barely begun to grieve the loss of one special moment when we must grieve another. But those moments are not really lost, they live on in the memory of the heart. There we hold them to remember on another day when special times are scarce.

Everyone...awaited the decisive moment.

(2 Maccabees 15:20)

CHANGE

Just when we finally get some stability and control in our lives, something changes and our world seems foreign and our days uncertain.

As we live, we come to discover that the only constant is change itself. On this we can depend: Life is change and change is life.

Life is a constant death-and-resurrection experience for us. It is composed of many cycles of endings and beginnings. It is a continual metamorphosis of our physical, emotional, and intellectual selves. Life is growth of the soul through change.

Perhaps the most obvious change is that of our physical being. We welcome the growth that moves us from birth to adulthood. Each day we grow stronger, taller, better able to care for ourselves. Sometimes we do not understand the growth that is happening to us, and we become frightened by it. This can happen to us at puberty, menopause, and other times of physical change.

As we mature in life, our emotional selves are also in transition. Like a two-edged sword, on the one hand we want to change emotionally to be able to enter the world of adulthood; on the other hand we resist any change that will burden us with grown-up responsibilities. This resistance can occur at any age.

Intellectually, we tend to play both sides. We are in favor of mind expansion and the entertainment of new ideas and different perspectives — for others. For ourselves, we know what we think, we are sure about what we believe, and we would just as soon keep it that way.

Change is difficult and sometimes filled with fear of the unknown and unexpected. We seem to prefer the actual — even if it is miserable — to something that might be better but must be acquired through painful change.

We find ourselves resisting change because our familiarity with the status quo gives us the security of knowing on what we can count. Yet, the status quo is but an illusion. When we least expect it, life has changed into something different than what it was, and we are confronted once again with the unwelcome task of adjustment.

To seek change of its own sake is not effective living. When change becomes our goal instead of the means toward growth, we may become irresponsible and fickle. Life-giving change comes to us when we allow nature to take its course.

In the process of growth through change there is first a period of disintegration in which we let go of what has been. Then comes a period of painful transition, a sort of limbo stage, in which we feel lost and may behave strangely. Finally, we enter a period of integration of the old with the new. This phenomenon repeats itself moment by moment throughout our lives.

If all is in transition, if life itself is change, then what will be the landmark that will guide us? What will be the anchor that will hold us steadfast? What will be the belief that will keep us faithful?

We must cleave to the constant of the "I Am" who is God. The God within each of us is the Alpha and the Omega, the beginning and the end. He is all. Yet, ours is a living God, a dynamic and everlasting Being who calls us toward growth, unfoldment, development, and evolution.

To resist inevitable change is to stagnate, to become stale, and to cease being fruitful. To will the will of God is to let go of our tenacious control over what is and allow what comes of God.

Surely I, the LORD, do not change....

(Malachi 3:6)

17

CHOICES

We determine who we will be tomorrow by the choices we make today. Our character and our way of life depend on the moment-by-moment decisions we make concerning what we will think and what we will do. We cannot escape the consequential nature of our actions.

Sometimes we live as though each day was a life unto its own, without the influences of days gone by. Yet, it is only when we encounter the consequence of our behavior that we remember it came by way of choice.

Choices confront us constantly, and the ones for which we opt are the living stones of the houses we build. Slowly but surely we become what we are by doing what we do. Our behavior breeds new life each time it is repeated, and each repetition gets its impetus from the time before.

It seems simple enough. All we have to do is choose good over evil. But it is not that simple. Often choices are not clear to us, and the good we choose may turn out to be evil disguised as good. We are attracted to evil not because we want to embrace evil as such but because it appears good to us. If evil alternatives were to expose themselves to us as such, we would probably reject them immediately. Instead, evil hides by camouflaging itself as good. It avoids a naked confrontation with us because it knows it would not otherwise have a chance. It takes on the identity of good in order to steal past the gates of our consciences.

Once the choice for evil is made, albeit inadvertently, the snow-ball of habit begins to roll downhill, becoming almost impossible to stop. Not only do we pay dearly for our choice by what we ultimately become, but also we lose control of our lives as the forces of habit assume more and more prerogative over our choice-making.

Habit is not in and of itself bad. It can save us from having to make choices constantly about everyday matters and thus free us to concentrate on more important affairs. It is only when the habit we have developed is detrimental to our lives that it becomes an enemy with which to contend.

If habit grows from repetition, then it dies from lack of repetition. But we must do much more than just try to stop our bad habits. We will not win over temptation by fighting it. In fact, the more we fight it on our own, the more involved we become in the problem.

It is said that only habit can overcome habit — which means that if we want to rid ourselves of one, we must discard it for another that is even more important to us. Its value to us must be such that it captivates our minds. Only then will we be willing to let go of one for the other.

We are not asked to turn our backs on the world; rather, we must learn to appreciate it for what it is. We *are* asked, however, to choose the higher joys in life and to follow the deepest desires of our hearts.

The curative process, then, involves more than a transfer of attention to good. It necessitates a turning to a power greater than ourselves. It requires that we fasten ourselves to this power and allow it to carry us. This greater power is God, nothing less. To him we must surrender ourselves. We must pledge our allegiance and dedicate our lives.

> **Only in God be at rest, my soul...**
> **He only is my rock and my salvation,**
> **my stronghold; I shall not be disturbed.**
> **(Psalm 62:6-7)**

COMING HOME

L ike the homing pigeon that returns to its point of origin, the
    lonely soul seeks to come home. This instinctual return is
    not an easy one. We may travel fast and hard and be far from
our abode. The basic yearning for our source is countered by our
hypnotic infatuation for the shallow and the temporal. We sometimes lose our way.

Immersed in the frantic business of false living, we believe
ourselves important and well-placed. Doing has taken the place of
being, and the branches become independent of the vine. In the
name of goodness and charity we are dedicated to our work. But if
our work becomes paramount to life's purpose, we sink into
despair. We are fortunate, then, if through the noise of the city the
soul hears the call, "Come home, come home."

We live in a world of pain, suffering, and trouble, with matters
seemingly getting worse all the time. We are overwhelmed by the
depression that comes from helplessness, and sometimes we just
want to give up. We — all of us — are a broken people, a wounded
world. Anxiety, hostility, aggression, competition, and pride —
these are the states in which we find ourselves. Yet, amid the
anguish of disharmony and the cruelty of apathy, amid the pain of
poverty and the devastation of war, the soul hears the call, "Come
home, come home."

But in spite of the yearning to return, we are afraid to go home.
We are afraid to stop running, lest we discover who we really are

and who we are not. We are afraid that if we cease to do, we will cease to exist. We are afraid to let go of illusions and face realities. We are afraid to admit our limitations and to realize our potentialities. We are afraid to be intimate with ourselves and with our God.

Our souls are called home to rest, to re-create, to reconnect with their sources. Going home does not mean that we withdraw or quit or retreat from life in defeat. Rather, it restores us so that we can learn once again to be. At home we do not have to be afraid. We can relax and put down our guard. We don't have to pretend that we are someone we are not. We don't have to struggle because we are already free.

At home we can take off our shoes, get comfortable, laugh at ourselves, and cry those tears we've been holding back. We can dance and sing and be silly without being criticized or judged. We can rest our tired bones and heal our broken hearts. We can take the time to remember and grieve, and we can take the time to play and have fun.

At home we can open ourselves to receive and enjoy the glory of God through nature. Here we are safe, cared for, loved. Here we can pray and commune. At home we dare to be vulnerable and intimate, for here we are understood. At home no one expects us to be other than who we are — the children of God.

May the LORD grant each of you...a home in which you will find rest.

(Ruth 1:9)

COMMITMENT

We are afraid to commit, lest we miss out on something; yet our noncommitted way of life may leave us missing out on everything.

Commitment is one of the most feared words in the English language because of the images it conjures up. We hear it and imagine it involves a total investment that closes off all other possibilities. We think that it means being placed in some impossible situation, or we see it as complete surrender of ourselves with no possibility of return.

Commitment frightens us because it means we must let go of all options, save one. We believe that when we commit we lose myriads of other opportunities open to us. Commitment means that we have to work within the limits of that to which we have committed. It means staying when we'd rather go, connecting when we'd rather stay loose, sinking roots when we'd rather move on. In short, our fear of commitment has to do with our fear of losing our freedom.

What we have yet to learn, however, is that freedom which is fearful of involvement in life is not true freedom. In fact the only freedom we come to enjoy is ours as a result of the choices we make in life. As we choose between alternatives, and as we decide between possibilities, we move from the disintegrating force of duality toward the integrating force of commitment.

Whether we commit to a person, a mission, or to God, we are bonded with the object of our commitment. It is not a bond that traps us, but rather one that frees us to fulfill our potential as human beings.

Our commitment carries with it an implied promise to invest ourselves entirely. Our promise is to focus on who we are and to concentrate on what we can do to fulfill the commitment.

To remain in a marriage, for example, or the priesthood or on a mission, we must be willing to apply all our resources to the best of our abilities. Commitment calls forth our full effort and extracts from us our finest contribution.

It is true that commitment requires of us the courage of self-denial. It sometimes means sacrifice and struggle, and it always means letting go of our desire to have it all.

The paradox is that as we dare to choose, as we risk to decide, as we dare to commit, we are liberated from the death of surface living. By our commitment we are granted the peace of purposefulness and the joy of a meaningful life. In our commitment we become single-minded and surefooted in our endeavor. Through our commitment we release the energy of concentration.

Our purpose becomes that to which we have committed, and the meaning of our lives becomes the fulfillment of our promises.

The kingdom of heaven is like a merchant searching for fine pearls. When he finds a pearl of great price, he goes and sells all that he has and buys it.
(Matthew 13:45-46)

CRISIS

It may come on gradually or it may appear seemingly from nowhere, but all of a sudden we are face-to-face with a crisis.

Our first reaction is to panic because we are never prepared for crises as we may be for other problems in life. We are overtaken by a fear of the unknown. Our imagination runs wild, and we anticipate the worst that can happen.

In our panic we may turn to some form of substance abuse or we may delve into other forms of debasement in an attempt to escape the reality that confronts us. As a result we may become immobilized and worthless to ourselves and to others.

Our anxiety symptoms may be of a physical nature (like indigestion or insomnia), or they may be of a psychological nature (like preoccupation with the past or an inability to think clearly).

Usually a crisis makes us realize that from this point on our lives will never be the same, and awareness of this intensifies our insecurity and raises our anxiety.

Sometimes in the cloud of confusion we make rash judgments as we search for immediate solutions to the crisis. Another reaction is to feel that the crisis is confirmation of our failure as persons. We then think that there is not much sense in trying to resolve the crisis, and we fall into inaction and self-pity.

How a crisis affects us does not depend so much on its nature as it does on how we react to it. Our attitude toward whatever happens to us makes the difference between succumbing to the crisis or overcoming it.

The word *crisis* comes from the Greek word for *decision*. A crisis presents us with an opportunity for decision.

As we face our crisis, we decide how we will respond to it. Recognizing what is really important to us, we make a decision on the best course of action to take. We also decide whether we will allow the crisis to bury us or whether we will turn it into a life-giving experience.

Crisis is also defined as "the turning point for better or worse...the decisive moment..." in a person's life. Which way it turns depends on us.

Although it brings risk and danger in our lives, a crisis may also offer us an opportunity for growth. By testing us beyond measure, it provides us with new strength and courage to overcome.

To confront a crisis and then to move through it toward resolution, we must have the strength and the courage to change our set ways of looking at things and our established pattern of behavior. When we let go of the way we have expected our lives to be, we can adjust to this new reality and make the best of it.

With courage we enter into the crisis, allowing ourselves to experience it fully. We do not try to avoid it or diffuse it. With courage we dare to ask for help from a friend or a professional in dealing with the crisis. Someone who really cares and is willing to listen to us can be helpful in reducing our anxiety, clarifying our confusion, and soothing our hurt. Ultimately, of course, it is up to us to resolve our own crisis.

Our courage derives from the strength within ourselves. It is not a fearlessness of the crisis; rather, it is a conviction that we have been given what we need to adjust and to persevere. It is a faith that takes us through the pain and the fear into a renewed confidence and a strong sense of self.

When you make a decision, it shall succeed for you,
and upon your ways the light shall shine.

(Job 22:28)

DESERT
EXPERIENCES

In the desert of life we come of age. We enter into this wilderness feeling lost and confused, lonely and abandoned. Formerly so self-sufficient and so capable of taking care of ourselves, now our hands are empty and our hearts are filled with grief.

The word *desert* means a land that has been cut off, separated, abandoned, and this is where we suddenly find ourselves.

Perhaps we have become sick from the neglect of our physical selves; we may be tired from overwork and little play; or we may have been preoccupied with things external, not living according to the calling of our higher selves. Maybe we have just forgotten to take the time to pray. Whatever the reason, we have been depending on ourselves as our primary source and have become separated from our life forces.

In this arid environment we become dry and desolate. Try as we may, we cannot reach the wellspring of our souls. We are thrown by necessity back onto ourselves, but we are no help at all.

There seems to be no relief from this hell of separation. The more control we lose over our lives, the more meaningless everything seems, and the more we try to control. What used to be ordered and manageable is falling apart, disintegrating before our eyes. We are losing our well-established roles; we are being confronted with change faster than we can adjust to it.

But even now, standing in the middle of the barren desert, we refuse to let go of our illusion of control and self-sufficiency. We huff and puff, still believing that somehow through the power of our will, our control, our effort, we can tame the desert. But the desert guards its secrets jealously from those who see it as another frontier to conquer. It laughs at our attempts to figure it out and bring it under control. The lesson of the desert is that we are not in control of everything.

It is only when we surrender to the desert experience, to our powerlessness, and to our utter dependence on the God of the desert that we have a chance at survival.

This does not mean that we are to turn into passive victims. It indicates that we must first acknowledge our weakness so that we may lean on the strength of God; that we admit our fear so that we may receive the courage of God; that we deem ourselves poor on earth so that we may be enriched by the treasures of heaven; and that we declare ourselves lost so that we may take the leading hand of God.

In the desert we will not see God. There we must depend on our faith, trust, and love of him. It is miserable to seek God and not find him, but in the desert the heart believes in God even in his absence.

The desert experience becomes for us a turning point. In the desert we discover that it is not God who has abandoned us, but we who have abandoned him through our neglect and our way of life. Desert experiences teach us to let go of all that blocks our love for God. We even let go of that God whom we have invented to satisfy our needs and attach ourselves to the God whom we love for his own sake.

When we release our control over life, we gain what life offers to us. We gain access to possibilities that would have been stifled under our control. When we surrender to the desert, we open ourselves to the adventure of life.

In the desert we change our priorities. That which was formerly so important to us is not so now; and that to which we gave little attention before becomes paramount.

The desert teaches us to detach from that which is not necessary.

We put aside the luxury of idle thinking and feed instead on the simple meal of love and dependence.

In the desert we become realistic. We do not hold out for that which we would prefer; we are forced to make the best of what we have. The desert teaches us to treasure every moment we are alive. It shows us how fragile life is and how much tender loving care it requires.

In the desert we let go of all that is not of God and attach to everything that is. We begin to learn what life is really all about: loving God with all our hearts and being open to his love for us.

I will lead her into the desert
and speak to her heart.

(Hosea 2:16)

DESPAIR

Sometimes it seems as though the whole world is falling down on us. Everything goes wrong all at once and we don't know where to turn. When all around us seems to totter; when dreams are broken, and hope is dashed against the rocks; when life seems tedious and demanding, we are tempted to despair.

These are times of anguish. In the midst of our troubles, we feel the urge to run away, to check out, to put our minds on hold, or even to cease existing, in hope that our painful problems will disappear. It is at this time of desperation that we can choose to run toward the void of unreality, escaping into the prison of alcohol or other drug abuse, or to wallow in the fantasy of irresponsibility and disconnectedness.

Through the noise of our confusion and the dizziness of our thought, we hear the words of well-meaning friends: "Have faith," they say, "everything will be all right."

Have faith in whom? Are we supposed to believe that God will come charging in on a white cloud and rescue us from our pain and suffering? Have faith in what? Are we being asked to believe that everything will return to normal and our troubles will disappear if only we believe that they will?

Our experience tells us that bad things do happen to people and merely having faith that they don't will not change the situation. The twisting knot in our chests and the draining tension in our heads are very real to us. Words tend to sound empty and unreal at times like these. Even when we are advised to consider heavenly things, our troubled waters do not recede. Comparing our state of life with the glory of the eternal doesn't help much either.

We are needful of practical help based on the nature of our humanity, and yes, on our faith in God. But having faith doesn't mean that we are to ask God for extra help to get us through the difficult times. Having faith in God means believing that he has already gifted us with all that we need to confront the adversities of life.

One such gift is our ability to divide and conquer the crises which come our way. When we forget to use this gift, we allow too much stimuli, too many problems, too lengthy segments of time, to enter our consciousness and overwhelm us. Our greatest temptation is to despair in the face of what appears to be more than we can handle.

Jesus himself (in Matthew 6:34) breaks down the unsurmountable into portions which we are equipped to handle mentally, emotionally, physically, and spiritually.

We must scale down the crisis to fit our abilities to cope with it. Instead of the year, we consider the moment; instead of the staircase, we consider the step; instead of the problem, we consider a part of the problem.

Another gift is the ability to exorcise the phantoms of the future and to focus on the present moment and all that we can bring to it. The present moment is all that is given to us, and living it effectively is all that is expected of us.

When we can focus in this way, we tap a tremendous reservoir of human capabilities. We gain the composure necessary to make appropriate decisions; we become aware of our fear and anxiety, expressing these emotions without falling victim to them; and we experience a surge of energy that fuels our body according to our needs.

It is at our time of pain and trouble that we can choose to rest in what is real. To rest does not preclude "getting away" for a while to set our bearings. It does not mean we choose pain over pleasure or confusion over reasoning. To rest does not mean that we understand what is going on in our lives or even that we have hope in the future. It merely means that we are willing to wait through the uncertainty of the night, believing in the dawn.

What makes the wait so lonely is the separation that we feel, sometimes even from God. We cannot pray, nor do we even feel like praying. Yet, we allow and accept the separation as part of where we are this moment, believing, without evidence, that at the level of the soul there is no separation. This sense of good and wholeness that we experience at the core of ourselves is that to which we hold when there is nothing else. This is the masthead to which we cling as our ship is tossed and turned by stormy seas.

We have no evidence that we will be all right. We are given no assurance that the winds will be quieted. We have only our commitment to hang on, to wait, and to choose not to despair.

We are afflicted in every way, but not constrained; perplexed, but not driven to despair.

(2 Corinthians 4:8)

ENDINGS
AND
BEGINNINGS

S unset, sunrise, endings and beginnings — these we celebrate.
But as the day is done and the season runs its course, we
feel the grief of separation and the agony of change. We are
saddened to have to say good-bye to that which was and is no
more.

Even as we face the reality that something significant to us has
ended, we tend to deny it. We are afraid of closure because of its
finality. Yet, to cling to the ghost of yesterday is to preclude the
newness of today. Our instinct to survive compels us to maintain
the status quo, but our survival as transitional beings depends on
letting go.

We can transcend the pain of termination by giving it a meaning
and a purpose in our lives. As we ritualize our endings through
gesture or ceremony, we come to grips with the reality of it all.

We celebrate that which is ending by giving it a place in our
hearts. We may be experiencing the ending of a life, the ending of
a way of life, the ending of an era, the ending of a relationship, the
ending of our youth, the ending of a job, the ending of a project.
We may let go of them in actuality, but we hold them dearly in
memory.

We celebrate endings by openly acknowledging their passing
and by experiencing all of our emotions. We celebrate endings by

crying the tears of loss and by releasing regrets and disappointments over what might have been. We celebrate endings by forgiving ourselves and others for the wrong we did or the good we failed to do.

We celebrate endings by choosing to build on them rather than letting them stifle or otherwise limit us and by respecting the past as an integral part of the present. We celebrate endings by trusting God with our beginnings.

As we wake to the light of the new day, we celebrate the gift of another chance, another go at life. Now we are at the threshold of a new adventure. Now we embark on a journey into dark and uncharted waters. Now we rely on faith to see us through. This is a trust in God's love for us and in his sacred plan for the world.

Slowly, and not without trepidation, we move toward the challenge of the day, believing that we have been given what we will need to meet it. We call up from within the courage to persevere in the face of uncertainty and not fall into the temptation to return to the familiar but illusory security of the past.

We celebrate beginnings with hope and expectation of what is to come. We celebrate with confidence in ourselves and reliance on the comfort of God. We celebrate the plans we make and the resolutions we mean to keep. We celebrate beginnings by turning over control to God and risking all on the belief that he works for our good and for the fulfillment of our lives.

Behold, I am coming soon....I will give to each according to his deeds. I am the Alpha and the Omega, the first and the last, the beginning and the end.

(Revelation 22:12-13)

ENCOURAGEMENT

Sometimes we feel all alone, abandoned and worthless. We have lost confidence in ourselves. We are discouraged. Left alone, we will sink into the pit of despair; but through the encouragement of those who care, we can rediscover the energy of our own souls. It is at such times — when we do not believe in ourselves — we are buoyed by the belief others have in us.

We are encouraged by those who believe in our wholeness even when we are broken; by those who value us even when we feel worthless; and by those who challenge us to risk even when we are afraid. We come to discover our strength of heart when we allow others to discover it in us. And just as we can receive the gift of encouragement, we can also offer it to others.

Courage means the power to act from our hearts. We *en-courage* others by helping them tap the power of their own inner resources. We help others to believe in their abilities, to accept and learn from their mistakes, and to accept their limitations and imperfections.

We encourage others when we accept them unconditionally, give them the freedom to change or to remain the same, recognize their efforts and their improvements and focus on their strengths and assets. Most of all, we encourage others when we love them and believe in their ability to love us back.

Therefore, encourage one another....
(1 Thessalonians 5:11)

FAITH

Sometimes God is silent. Cry as we may for his attention, not a sound, not a stir, comes from him. This may happen because of doubt and hopelessness. It is then that our enemies advance toward the fortress of our souls. Fear threatens our right flank, while despair charges at our left. At such times it appears that we have been forgotten in our plight, abandoned in the midst of the war of life.

Sometimes what appears to be God's silence is really an insensitivity we have acquired because we have neglected God, and this has caused us to lose contact. In such a case we need to reestablish our communication with him.

There are other times, however, when we encounter God's silence in spite of our constant attention to him in prayer. Abruptly, we lose our grip on life. Where there was light, there is now darkness; where there was security, there is now anxiety; where there was direction, there is now confusion.

What makes us feel so insecure? Where are the feelings of joy and ecstasy in prayer? The desert through which we walk is dry and desolate; we are confused and lost.

God's silence forces us to make a choice. We may decide to panic or despair because what we had counted on is not there, or we may decide to call on our faith to see us through the night.

But what is faith? It is not a total and blind acceptance of doctrinal creeds. It is not the contradicting of reason, nor the tasting of the opium of sentimentality, nor the drinking of the inebriating cup of fanatical zeal. It is not acquiescent and passive observance of religious ritual and routine.

Faith is not a mere mental exercise, and it is not an emotional high or a mechanical obedience. Faith is a vibrant, provocative, even revolutionary, state of being that is born of communion with God. To have faith is to believe in something beyond ourselves, something that transcends our limited view of reality and is not manifested to us except through the eye of the soul.

Faith is not just believing in miracles either. It is a conviction that there is a higher order than the order of our senses.

Faith does not necessarily do away with the hardness of life. It is a belief that helps us to persevere in the face of all contradictions. Through faith, we dare to have confidence in the goodness of God and his loving grace, even when we do not feel his presence. This focus on the source of all good enables us to affirm life despite its difficulties.

But we cannot have or obtain faith if we refuse to pray — because prayer is a most important conduit to the source of faith. The *manner* in which we pray is less important than the *act* of prayer itself. We need to pray even when we don't feel like praying.

When we pray we discover that God never left us. Once we strip ourselves of doubt, we are left with nothing but our faith in God. When we can no longer depend on the fruit, we come to know the Tree. We may feel empty, but there is a part of us that clings to the thread that connects our souls to God.

No one of us escapes the dark night of the soul and no one of us is without the internal light. Our hearts keep beating to the rhythm of God and our souls march on in love. Even though the world around us seems hopeless, we maintain our hope; and although we find no evidence on which to place our faith, we continue to believe.

Your faith has saved you. Go in peace....

(Mark 5:34)

FEELINGS

To be fully responsible (accountable for our actions) in life, we must go beyond fulfilling our obligations and performing our duties. We must also utilize our ability to answer to life and to those around us with all of our humanness.

We have been taught to be responsible for families, households, jobs, governments, and even for the propagation of the Faith. We have taken our jobs so seriously that we have not allowed ourselves to get in touch with, much less to express, that part of ourselves we call our emotions or *feelings*.

What is this conditioning we have undergone which has us living more as machines than as human beings? It has to do with fear. We have come to believe that emotions are tantamount to weakness, to vulnerability, and to lack of control.

Many of us believe that our emotions are like the molten lava that erupts uncontrollably from the mysterious depths of a volcano. No wonder we suppress our feelings, lest they get out of hand and do damage to ourselves or others.

Were we to consider emotions not as sudden outbursts but rather as intentional communications revealing our identities and our tasks in life, then we would understand that their identification and expression are essential parts of our human personalities.

The persons who love and interact with us on a regular basis need this form of communication from us. By fully experiencing and then expressing our feelings to them, we share our entire selves, we build better understanding, and we bond firmer relationships.

We alone are responsible for our emotions and for the actions which are prompted by them. We absorb information through our senses, and we interpret this information based on our life experiences; then we decide on the appropriate feeling to express that interpretation.

After choosing the feeling, we choose what action we will perform to express the feeling. Of course, all this happens very quickly within us and is less mechanical than it sounds. Nevertheless, it is sequential and it is in our control.

If we really want to be in control, we must assume responsibility for our feelings and how we express them. We will need courage to express all of our feelings, including those of compassion, affection, fear, confusion, vulnerability, exaltation, and intimacy. We must not confine ourselves only to those few feelings with which we seem to feel comfortable.

Emotions are inherent in our humanity. They are a language with which we may communicate to those around us, either constructively or destructively. The choice is ours.

> **When Jesus saw her [Mary] weeping...he became perturbed and deeply troubled.**
>
> **(John 11:33)**

FEMININE INFLUENCE

Within every man there is a woman.

For most of our lives, however, we men deny her existence. In our attempts to reject her presence, we resort to ridicule. We try to suppress any traces of her, even killing or dying — in senseless bravado — to prove her nonexistence in us. Yet, all the while, the feminine influence remains within us, calling us toward a more creative life, a fuller sense of self, and a spirituality known only to those whole enough to grasp it.

We all have qualities of the opposite sex, not only biologically but also psychologically — which is evident if we closely examine our attitudes and feelings. Wholeness necessitates that we men balance within ourselves both our masculine and our feminine sides.

In our society this has not been easy. The feminine side of us is often underdeveloped because we condemn femininity in men. Even as children we are ridiculed as "sissies" when we express any characteristics that are traditionally reserved for the feminine gender. So we suppress any signs of this real but unwelcome side of ourselves and begin to exaggerate our masculine side. The result has been a gross imbalance of our humanness.

Forbidden to delve into our feminine side, we men are ill-prepared to understand or deal with the women in our lives. They continue to be mysterious and strange to us.

We end up projecting onto women the femininity we deny within ourselves, and then they become for us what we cannot be for ourselves. But our expectations are often unmet, and outward disharmony erupts between the sexes because there is inward disharmony between the sexes.

When we men stop repressing our feminine traits, when we allow the Eve within us to live, our more positive masculine traits will be manifested. Where our masculine side might reflect courage when balanced with vulnerability, it stands alone as bravado. Where objectivity may benefit us when balanced with warmth, it manifests itself as insensitivity.

Strength without gentleness becomes sheer dominance; decisiveness without patience becomes impulsiveness; industriousness without purpose becomes control; power without compassion becomes cruelty; justice without mercy becomes vengeance; physicalness without tenderness becomes force; sexuality without sensuality becomes mechanical; and faith without spirituality becomes religiosity.

If we men fully accept this feminine influence, it will lead us to discover our emotions and will teach us to express them without shame. It will guide us to the door of receptiveness. It will teach us to value the intuitive, the seemingly illogical, and the mysterious. It will show us how to appreciate nature and help us to become humble. It will journey with us into the realm of the unconscious and will prompt us to let go and experience whatever comes.

The feminine influence described here holds the key to our souls and unlocks our creativity, our spirituality, and our reservoir of love. Every man, therefore, should allow for the inner marriage of his masculine and feminine sides, and he should let the issue of that marriage become his wholeness.

> **God created man in his image...**
> **male and female he created them.**
>
> **(Genesis 1:27)**

FOLLOWING CHRIST

C ome, follow me.
In an age of confusion and a world seemingly without purpose, how comforting it is to hear these words of invitation and assurance. Yet, many of us are afraid to follow because too much may be asked of us.

"If you wish to be perfect, go, sell what you have and give to [the] poor, and you will have treasure in heaven. Then come, follow me" (Matthew 19:21).

These words Jesus spoke to the young man who wanted to be whole. Yet, the man left feeling profound sadness because he had too much to give up. He would have wholeness but was not willing to pay the price for it. His wealth made him poor. Do we not also walk away in sorrow because we will not let go of that which we possess? Do we not also choose the lesser good, the mundane, and the perishable?

It would be easier if the call toward wholeness was simply to let go of our material possessions and our monetary wealth. We could make a few donations and be home free. But it becomes a bit more difficult when we are asked to let go of our precious attachments as proof that we are willing to heed the call.

Our attachments can indeed be material, but more often they have to do with obsessions, addictions, and other substitutes for the treasure in heaven, which is the true desire of the soul. This treasure in heaven is wholeness, the integration and completion of our identity in the eyes of God. The price we must pay is the letting go of *anything* that encumbers the spirit or blocks the light.

Our "possessions" may include control over our lives and our environment; fear of vulnerability, risk, or surrender; even security, pride, superiority, piety, or power. All of these are not harmful to the spirit in and of themselves; it is our hold on them that binds us to a lesser life.

Consider the meaning of "Go, sell what you have and give to the poor...." Why not just let our possessions go? How can we *sell* them?

Could it mean that when we sell a possession we are exchanging it for something that is more beneficial at the time and which can be more readily transferred or given away? We can, for example, sell a piece of furniture for money that can be given to the economically poor for the food that they badly need. In the same manner we can sell our control for some spontaneity and warmth which we, in turn, can give away to the emotionally poor who need it badly. We can sell our fear of vulnerability, risk, and surrender for the intimacy which we can give away to those in need of it. In this manner we can go on converting that which hinders the spirit to that which gives more abundant life to others.

With empty hands we can receive that which will be given for the journey toward wholeness. With detachment from the possessions which blind, deafen, and otherwise cripple us spiritually, we are able to attach to that which gives us comfort and direction, meaning and purpose, belonging and wholeness.

Feel the pull into the light. Surrender to the inner life. Hear the voice that calls to us.

Come, follow me.

(Matthew 19:21)

FORGIVENESS

From the tree of torture, mixed with groans of agony, came the plea of a gentle soul: "Father, forgive them, they know not what they do" (Luke 23:34).

Jesus had spoken about forgiveness in the past, but now he was going beyond the mere cancellation of debts and the letting go of resentments. Now, even as others tortured and killed him, he was giving them the benefit of the doubt. In fact, this man of compassion was pleading on their behalf with God.

This kind of forgiveness is extraordinary, to be sure; yet it is the kind of forgiveness to which we are called by our faith, hope, and love.

Christ's words of forgiveness are a manifestation of faith in a merciful God who gathers up the pieces and restores the broken vessel (see Psalm 31:12). They are a manifestation of hope in the return of another who once was dead but is now alive again, who once was lost and now is found (see Luke 15:24). They are a manifestation of love that sets aside revenge and goes beyond justice: a love that abrogates bondage and releases prisoners (see Matthew 18:27).

No forgiveness can be genuine or effective without first facing the reality of the injury and experiencing its consequences, including the feelings of hurt, anger, and resentment. Beyond that, it is a matter of deciding to cancel that which is owed.

This would seem enough, but now Jesus adds to it understanding and compassion. Not only are we to forgive injuries large and small, but we are to consider that those who have hurt us were probably doing the best they could do with what they had at the time.

In effect, our prayer of forgiveness must be the same as Jesus': "Please, God of mercy and love, give them a second chance. They have acted from their blindness. Do not give up on them." Our plea for their forgiveness must carry with it the mercy of a higher justice, the hope that they can learn from their mistakes, and the love to set them free.

Such forgiveness neither affects the pain inflicted nor alters the consequences suffered. It does not invite the injury to be repeated. Forgiveness enables us to transcend barriers and bridge schisms that have developed from past injuries. Forgiveness prepares the way for love.

Father, forgive them, they know not what they do.
(Luke 23:34)

GOD'S WILL

A t times it seems as if life is but a continuous struggle between following our will or the will of God.

Much of our religious training has taught us to suppress our will in favor of God's. The need to suppress the will implies that what we want runs counter to what God would have for us. So denial of self-interests, wishes, or desires, it would appear, is tantamount to doing the will of God.

The result of this approach to better living, however, is that it sets us up as separate and apart from God. It puts us at opposite poles with the Divine. It is as if we are wild horses that need to be broken and domesticated before we can be of any use to God or to his world.

This "father-knows-best" attitude which has been handed down to us through the ages has given us a harsh image of God. Many of us have imagined God as an authoritarian, always ready to punish those who disobey his will. Some of our feelings of resentment, hostility, inhibition, and self-rejection have come from this childish image of God.

And our image of God has not been helped by those who have told us that the bad happenings in our lives are a part of his will. For example, when we lose a loved one through death, we are told by some to "accept the will of God." We who have heard this kind of talk, especially children, come to believe that if God wills this on us and our loved ones, then he is not a God of love and mercy but just some power-hungry ruler who demands to have his way.

Could it be that God's will has nothing to do with specifics but rather with the overall direction of the world? Maybe several paths are open to us, all of which would fall within his will.

There are some basic assumptions we can make about all this. God wills health and life, peace and joy, truth and courage, for us. He wills union with us and love among us. Most of all, God wills that we come to know, through prayer and contemplation, that our wills are completely in agreement with his.

Thomas Merton wrote that it is not enough to do the will of God, we must will the will of God. But rather than accept that our wayward and rebellious will is at odds with the will of God and must be subdued and brought into line, God wants us to recognize the duality within ourselves. He would have us acknowledge openly to ourselves and to him that there is a part of us which wills the treasures of the world and a part of us which wills the higher good, the will of God. Our spiritual task is to become conscious of the latter and to focus on it so much that the other fades from our consciousness.

We spend too much mental time and energy suppressing the will of our lesser selves and trying to will God's will. Instead, we should enter into the chamber of our souls where, through prayer and contemplation, we discover that what God wills for us is our will too. In this discovery there is integration and peace. In these connected moments we get a glimpse of the God within, and we remember that we are God's life on earth.

**Your kingdom come,
your will be done,
on earth as in heaven.**

(Matthew 6:10)

GRATITUDE

Abba, dear Father, our world is filled with tragedy, and our lives are in the midst of despair. There is hunger, injustice, war, and abuse of nature all around us. Your children are hurting emotionally and physically.

Some of us are struggling with personal conflicts and the agony of life. Others of us suffer because we see the self-inflicted pain and destruction in the lives of others and feel helpless to reach them.

We do not curse you for the sickness of the world, Abba, but we thank you for the gifts of hope and perseverance with which we keep making our best efforts. We do not attribute the ugliness in the world to you, but we are grateful for the gifts of openness and appreciation through which we recognize the beauty in everything and everybody.

We do not hold you responsible for suffering and death, but we thank you for the gifts of grief and growth which also come our way. You do not cause others to hurt us, but you give the gift of forgiveness through which we can make whole our brokenness. You do not bring the injustice and cruelty that results from rampant apathy and an insane race for power and wealth, but you bring to us the gift of love which moves us toward a more excellent way.

Loving you, Abba, with all our hearts and with all our minds and with all our strength is the simple, single purpose of our souls. Our hearts burst with the joy of just being with you. The song of love we sing to you comes not only from our voices of prayer but also from our hands of service.

As we live our lives and face calamities and sorrows, as we enter the storm of confusion and lose our way, we know this: You are

God from whom we come and to whom we shall return. We belong to you, we hear your sweet and gentle calling, and we hasten to follow you wherever you may lead.

With great appreciation we receive the days you give to us. With deep faith we walk with you through hills and valleys. We thank you, Abba, for being God. We thank you for trusting us to live your life and to care for your world. We thank you for respecting us by giving us responsibility for ourselves and for our destiny. We thank you for your unconditional acceptance of us, and we thank you for a love that never dies.

> **Sing joyfully to the LORD, all you lands;**
> > **serve the LORD with gladness;**
> > **come before him with joyful song.**
>
> **Know that the LORD is God,**
> > **he made us, his we are;**
> > **his people, the flock he tends.**
>
> **Enter his gates with thanksgiving,**
> > **his courts with praise;**
>
> **Give thanks to him; bless his name,**
> > **for he is good,**
>
> **the LORD, whose kindness endures forever,**
> > **and his faithfulness, to all generations.**
>
> **(Psalm 100:1-5)**

GRIEF

G rief strikes us all. It comes to visit once in a while just to remind us that we are still fragile people. Healing does follow after death touches us, and we learn to adjust to a world without our deceased ones. But the truth is we never completely heal because we never totally adjust to the loss of a major love.

Such is the nature of loss that no matter how much time has passed and no matter how much life has been experienced, the heart of the bereaved will never be the same. It is as though a part of us also dies with the person we lose through death or other forms of permanent separation. We will be all right, but we will never be the same.

Grief touches our lives in various ways. Sometimes it enters through the door of our memory. A certain song, a certain fragrance, a certain picture, will remind us of how it used to be. Sometimes it brings a smile to the face, sometimes a tear.

Some may say that such remembering is not healthy, that we ought not to dwell on thoughts that make us sad. Yet the opposite is true. Grief revisited is grief acknowledged, and grief confronted is grief resolved.

But if grief is resolved, why do we still feel a sense of loss on the occasion of anniversaries and holidays and even when we least expect it? Why do we feel a lump in the throat even years after the loss? It is because healing does not mean forgetting and because moving on with life does not mean that we don't take a part of our lost loved one with us.

Of course, the intensity of the pain decreases over time if we allow grief to visit us from time to time. But if the intensity remains or if our lives are still dysfunctional years after our loss, we may be so thwarted that we need professional help.

Sometimes grief steals up on us. We'll feel an unexplained but profound sadness that clings to us for days. Then we'll recognize the grief and pray for the strength to go on. It's as though the ones we have loved and lost are determined not to be forgotten.

Grief doesn't want to get in the way of our living. It just wants to stop and chat sometimes. In fact, grief can teach us a few things about living that we would not have learned on our own.

Old grief can teach us over the years that if we try to deny the reality of a major loss in our lives, we end up having to deny life altogether. It can teach us that though the pain of loss is great, we must confront it and experience it fully or risk emotional paralysis.

Old grief can also teach us that we can survive even great losses and that, although our world is very different after a major loss, it is still our world and we must live in it. The time of grief can teach us that after we have been pruned by past losses, we can flourish again in season and bring forth the good fruit that comes, not in spite of loss, but because of it.

Grief can teach us that the loss of a loved one does not mean the loss of love; for love is stronger than separation and longer than the permanence of death.

Grief may leave us for a while, but it will be back again to remind us to confront our new reality and to grow and gain through loss and pain.

I will turn their mourning into joy,
I will console and gladden them after
their sorrows.

(Jeremiah 31:13)

HEALING

We are a wounded people in need of healing.

We have wounded one another with our power plays, our need to be right, our pride of righteousness, our sense of competition, and our need to win. We have wounded one another with our failure to listen, to accept, to cooperate, to understand, or to come together as one family under God.

We are wounded, and nothing short of the sweet salve of love will heal our painful wounds.

We are not unlike those people who came to the rugged mountainside hoping to hear the words that would ease the pain of life and give meaning to their days. (See Matthew 5:3-10.)

"Blessed are the poor in spirit," said the young teacher, **"for theirs is the kingdom of heaven."** Are we all not wealthy with holiness and goodness, are some of us not rich with the coin of power and prestige? Are there any beggars among us who dare to come with empty hands, open to what God would want to give us? What are the treasures to which we hold so dearly? "Let go," the teacher seemed to be saying, "release all that gets in the way of God's love for you and your love for one another." This is how he would have us heal — by making us poor and empty and needy of God and one another.

"Blessed are they who mourn, for they will be comforted," he said. What is it that we must mourn? It is anything that has died within us and around us. It is imperative, according to the teacher, that we see things as they are and not as we would have them be. This means that we cannot keep alive that which has died or changed in our lives. Mourning what has died means that we must endure the pain of loss; and as we mourn, we are comforted, made strong. It is the process of grief that brings about the healing. It is the sorrow that turns to joy.

"Blessed are the meek, for they will inherit the land," he continued. He was calling us to be lowly, humble, open to one another in all our reality. He was saying that we need to be unpretentious, unassuming, not weak or afraid of one another but mild, gentle, kind, cooperative, willing to be with and for one another. Healed of the disease of separation which comes from superiority, we then let go of the stress that comes of having to be better, stronger, more powerful, more spiritual, than the rest. We inherit the earth, that is, we inherit all that is real.

"Blessed are they who hunger and thirst for righteousness, for they will be satisfied." In other words we are healed from disintegration when we focus our entire selves on the ways of love. When we hunger and thirst for God, when we crave his will, then nothing else will do and everything else gets in the way. Nourished by the Spirit, our minds, our hearts, our bodies, and our souls move and act for God in the world.

"Blessed are the merciful, for they will be shown mercy," said the teacher. We block love when we hold resentment in our hearts. We get spiritually bogged down when we carry too many of the debts that others owe us. Only an attitude of forgiveness that goes beyond words can heal us of this wound. And we cannot wait for others to deserve or earn our forgiveness. It is a gift, pure and simple, and when we release others of their trespasses, we also release and heal ourselves.

"Blessed are the clean of heart, for they will see God." The pure in heart are not just those who merely behave well or attend church regularly. They are those who, for the most part, focus on God as the center of everything, who pray constantly — all in order to stay tuned to the will of God.

The pure in heart dedicate their entire selves to letting God live in them. They are not exempt from making mistakes, but because of their priorities they come back to where they need to be — which is to be with God.

Focusing on God, the pure in heart are able to feel God's unconditional love and to recognize the love others give in their own limited way. Focusing on God heals us because it pulls us together, integrates us as whole persons in whom God can take his abode.

"Blessed are the peacemakers, for they will be called children of God." The peace of which the teacher wrote did not necessarily mean less stress and more calm. It included conflict, confrontation, suffering, difficulty, and trouble. The peace of which he spoke comes not from the world around us but from the peace of God within us.

The peacemakers are not those who go along to get along; they are not those who hesitate to speak up because they don't want to cause trouble or make waves. (Peace at any price is no peace at all.) Those who dare to be called sons and daughters of God are those who have been healed of self-centeredness, those who are willing to include the other person in the realm of life. When God and his children are acknowledged, welcomed, and loved, there is healing and there is peace.

"Blessed are they who are persecuted for the sake of righteousness, for theirs is the kingdom of heaven." Here we are healed of the disease of cowardice. With the courage that comes of love, we die to self and to the ways of the world. We are choosing moment by moment the ways of God over the temporal and mundane, in spite of the pressures to conform or acquiesce.

> **Therefore...pray for one another, that you may be healed.**
>
> **(James 5:16)**

HOLY SPIRIT

Doves and winds and tongues of fire, how you touch our souls. You give us love, you give us strength, you consume us with your joy. What is your name whose gifts are holiness and peace? From whence do you come who bear the spark that ignites our lives?

You are the Spirit of the holy God. You are the One who was among us, was gone, and now returns within us. The love of God has become our center, our very heart. It is you who calms the storm that rages in our minds. It is you who holds our hand as we walk the waves of the deep unknown. It is you who gives meaning to our suffering and mends our broken selves.

We cannot merit your visit. We do not deserve your living presence. You come to us in freedom and in friendship, and you stay no matter what you find. It is only when we move to seize you as our possession or when we disregard you as the principle of our lives that we are deprived of your assistance.

We pray to prepare a place for the guest who comes our way, expecting nothing for ourselves, believing not in the power of our prayer but in the benevolence of your eternal love.

Come, Secret Friend, into our lives, be within us as we work and play and walk the streets of our mortality. Live in us as we touch the lives of friends, and even enemies. "You will show me the path to life, fullness of joys in your presence, the delights at your right hand forever" (Psalm 16:11).

Yet, the treasure of your presence is not for us alone. You come to us that we may come to you and that the issue of our love go out among those who know you not. The power which you promise to us is not the power of might. It is the power to love, the power to be open, the power to receive that which you bestow. Even our desire for your presence is a gift from you.

It is in our receptivity that you rejoice, for when we are open, you can fill our world with yourself. The secret of the power that comes is the openness of our souls. As our love for you overwhelms us, we offer to you the pieces of our illusion. We know that our love for you is manifested, not in our gift to you but in our willingness to receive your gift to us.

Come Spirit of Love. Come Spirit of Peace. Come Spirit of God. We wait for you as a lonely woman waits on the shore for her beloved, expectantly, hopefully, anticipating the joy and ecstasy of your sweet arrival.

It is through us that you come unto humanity. It is in us that you sow the seed of love. It is by us that the Spirit moves into the world.

How sad that we at times ignore your presence. You would remain forever, but we are unfaithful. We turn away in distraction. We neither talk with you nor feel your closeness. We forget how much we need you. We feel alone; and falling to our knees we pray for a receptive heart and patient mind. We renew our belief in the sureness of your words.

And behold, I am with you always, until the end of the age.

(Matthew 28:20)

HOPE

Our hope, even in our darkest moments, is to become the expression of God in the world.

The Incarnation, in which we place our greatest hope, happens because God breathes life into our souls and we, in turn, give human shape and dimension to the life of God. God becomes flesh and we become spirit.

God touches us and awakens in us a longing for more. He begins in us the search for our true direction, and we move toward the interdependence of the human and the divine.

Our hope moves us from shallow life to the core of our humanity where we discover the dynamic forces of God's love. Hope changes us from passive to active, from helpless to helpful.

It is not miracles we hope for when we look to God. We are not asking him to take over our lives. Our hope is placed in what has already been given to us: the courage to stay in the present moment and to use our total selves in the task of living. To live wholly as human beings is to invoke the God within us.

Hope is not a fixation we have on the future as we ignore and neglect the present. It is in the present moment that we hope. It is in the now that we commit ourselves to live according to our potential. Now is the time to open our hearts to the will of God. Now is the moment to respond to life with vigor and purpose.

There is a difference between hoping and holding on to our expectations. Hope opens us up to the movement of God; expectation imposes our own will onto life. When we choose to hope, we let go of those expectations that bind us to a lesser life.

Through hope we extinguish old ideas that new thoughts may be formed. Through hope we come to acknowledge inevitable endings and welcome the onset of new beginnings. Through hope we become vulnerable to the pruning of old ways that inhibit growth and invite a more fruitful harvest in our lives.

The pain and suffering that are part of life do not disappear by hoping; they give purpose and meaning and power to transform us.

It is not that we turn our backs on the actuality of evil when we hope. It is not just a blind faith in the power of goodness to which we hold. Hope is the spiritual energy with which we strive to overcome difficulty, resolve problems, and survive in our journey through the valley of darkness.

Hope is not flight from despair but confrontation with it, trusting in our ability to transcend it. "I have told you this so that you might have peace in me. In the world you will have trouble, but take courage, I have conquered the world" (John 16:33).

Hoping includes an element of risk in living. Rather than merely demanding what we would have, we are willing to embark on the great adventure of life, depending not on the illusion of the security which we provide but on the reality of God's presence in us. Risking with hope allows our freedom to create according to the will of God.

Sometimes we do not feel the presence of God. Not only have we let go of the world but now we feel as though God has let go of us. From this feeling of total abandonment comes a profound longing for God. This yearning from the abyss of nothingness is the beginning of hope. Then we find God in the midst of our emptiness, among the strangers whom we encounter in a lost world, and in the dawn that overcomes the night.

> **You are my refuge and my shield;**
> **in your word I hope.**

(Psalm 119:114)

JOY

Joy is where we find it. We cannot induce it like we often do our pleasure. We are not responsible for it like we are for our happiness. Joy is the hidden treasure which we discover in the most unlikely places.

Joy is not announced by trumpets, nor is it framed in lights. Rather, it is to be found in the common ordinary fabric of life. It is everywhere or it is nowhere. It is our perspective of the commonplace that makes the difference.

If we seek joy by running away from the nature of our humanness, we will never grasp it. If we search for joy only in the extraordinary or the supernatural and overlook it in the daily events of our lives, we will never find it. If we wait for joy only on the mountaintop while we are oblivious to it in the valley, it will never arrive.

The joy that arrives in the morning comes not in spite of the night but because of it. This is the paradox of joy. It is not to be found separate and apart from the pain of life but integrated with it as we live out our humanity.

Joy is the rose that blooms among the thorns. We find it in those experiences of life which complete us. It is the irritation that is soothed, the thirst that is quenched, the need that is met.

Joy comes to us when our sense of beauty is touched by a hummingbird as it flits among spring flowers. It comes to us when our sense of humor is tickled by the antics of a child. It comes to us when intimacy is awakened in us by the physical or emotional touch of another. Joy comes to us when our need for aloneness takes us into the desert, there to hear the sound of silence.

Joy is the cross that forms when our incomplete self finds completion at the hand of God's love. When we acknowledge our poverty, God bestows on us his kingdom. When we are broken and wounded, he gives us the strength to keep going and the remedy for healing. When we are last in the eyes of the world, he places us at his right hand. When we are starving for the food of heaven, he fills us and then gives us more that we may share.

When we are injured by others and begin to hate, he gives us the power to forgive and the humility to be forgiven. When we get lost in the forest of life and forget our way home, he calls our name out gently until we can focus on him once more in prayer.

When chaos, confusion, strife, and conflict rule our heart and the hearts of others, he reminds us that love is stronger than fear and that we are all children of one God. When we are misunderstood or judged by others, he lets us know that we are not alone.

When the beloved accepts the gift from the lover, there is completion and there is joy.

Remain in my love, just as I have kept my Father's commandments and remain in his love.
(John 15:10)

LIVING
THE
PRESENT
MOMENT

The present moment is when the flower blooms. It is the softness of a baby's cheek, the glory of the morning sun. It is the ecstasy of life.

Life is now, and yet we miss it because we are somewhere else. In our fantasies of tomorrow we are distracted from the present moment by desires of what should be. Our thoughts which dwell on yesterday tie us down to our regrets of what has been. But it is in the present moment that we find reality, for anything else is memory or illusion.

The reality is that we can live and move only in the present moment. The future or the past is out of our control. The failure to deal within the confines of this reality brings tension and irritability into our lives. Of course we may plan for tomorrow, and we may gain experience from yesterday, but it is today that offers opportunity. It is today that offers choices. It is today that offers peace.

The past, present, and future are all interrelated. Our present is an accumulation of our past, and our future will be the consequence of our present. Standing in the present we can learn from the past, and planning for the future we act accordingly in the present. Above all, we must be attentive to the moment at hand, for here is where we set our course.

We are not to forget our past or resist looking into the future. Memories and dreams are threads in the fabric of life. Rather, we must embrace our past and our potential and give it meaning in the present moment. When we live in the now of the present moment, we bring to bear all the power of our existence. We are awake to the world around us. We are wholly present to those whom we love. We hear the messages of life, and we respond in our totality. We take all the energy, interest, and enthusiasm that we have been given and invest it in the moment at hand.

But living in the present moment is also very frightening for us because to stay here we must admit that the now is all we really have. In the present moment we must be painfully honest about ourselves and our limitations. This is why we are tempted to linger over yesterday or long for tomorrow.

We have not been promised a wealth of time, good health, or happiness; yet sometimes we live as though these were stored away for us in quantity. In our lives we have perhaps squandered much time and opportunity and have taken for granted the gifts of body, mind, and spirit. Only by staying in the present moment do we acknowledge that we are truly poor. Our supply of life is extremely limited and must be measured by the spoonful.

In our assumption of tomorrows to come we also assume that life owes us a debt, a debt which we intend to collect. And as we inventory our yesterdays, we calculate the debts which others owe to us. But in the present moment we let go of expectations of what we have coming, and we cancel the indebtedness of others. In the present moment we have no credit, we hold no vouchers. We are dependent on life to "give us this day our daily bread."

Anticipations of the future may sound challenging and more exciting than a boring present, but they also demand of us achievement, performance, doing. The paradox is that when we stay in the present moment and remember who we are instead of what we do, we empower ourselves to live more effectively and successfully. We focus on what is required of us in the moment at hand and leave the consequences to develop as they will.

Our temptation is to flee from the present. In the past or future we find refuge from a painful reality we may be facing, or we run from the awesome responsibility of co-creating our own destiny. It is less threatening to us to remain oblivious to the present moment and just let life happen to us.

We are also separated from the present moment by fears of tomorrow. We forget that only by staying in the present moment do we retain any control over what we fear in the future.

The guilt of the past also preoccupies our minds with what we should have done or not done. Only in the mercy of the present moment can we forgive ourselves the wrongs we have done and hold ourselves accountable for what we are doing now.

The present moment is not just a particular instant in a continuous series of equivalent moments, but rather it is unique and special because it is the one and only time in which we enter into life. Yesterday is gone forever and tomorrow may never come. We need to seize the present moment and live it to the fullest. We must live life by the same measure in which God grants it to us — one moment at a time.

In him we live and move and have our being.
                                                          (Acts 17:28)

LONELINESS

At some point in our lives we all experience that profound loneliness that comes of facing a difficult time alone.

Even though we may be surrounded by others in the midst of our crisis, their supportive presence does not grace the sanctuary of our suffering.

There is a point beyond which no one can accompany us, even through empathy. From that moment on we must continue the journey by ourselves.

The compassion, the comfort, and the companionship of others have seen us through the gravest moments of our lives, yet the moment of our ordeal is a moment alone. Now we must bear the pain without the support of others, without their strength, without their presence. Now, from amid our fear and anguish, we reach out and there is no one there. Our friends disappear and even the members of our family who reach out to us in helpless desperation cannot touch us.

It is at this time of existential loneliness that we feel abandoned, empty, vulnerable. There is no place to turn but within to the secret places of our souls.

Having let go of our reliance on the world to protect us, having released our loved ones as our rescuers, we begin to discover the one and only source of our security. We come to know the God who will never leave us alone because he is a part of us.

This basic human loneliness, which cannot be relieved even by those who love us most, can become the reason why we turn back to God. It induces a thirst that can be quenched only at his fountain.

We must exonerate those whom we have expected to alleviate

this loneliness, for they cannot bring us relief. Theirs is but to walk with us to the door through which our souls must enter alone. It is then we will discover that we are not alone after all.

Behold, the hour is coming and has arrived when each of you will be scattered to his own home and you will leave me alone. But I am not alone, because the Father is with me.

(John 16:32)

LOVE

L ove is the color of the soul. With love we flourish, without it we wither and die.

Love is the life force. No wonder we crave it so. It is the energy that nurtures growth, the salve that brings healing to us when we are broken, and help when we are downtrodden.

We were born to love and be loved, and nothing short of love will fulfill us. Love is the key that unlocks our creativity. It is the spark that gives zest to our living. It is the purpose that gives us the will to endure.

We do not love without first being loved. Only after receiving the unconditional love of God do we begin to love ourselves. Having received love, we can give it to others.

If we seek aliveness, we need to love. If we seek fulfillment, completeness, wholeness, we need love — for love is the power of life. To live by love is to live in freedom.

Love will not save us from the pain of life, nor will it protect us from the sorrow of death. Love is the power of God within us that transcends pain and sorrow. From love comes the courage to persevere through the night and the faith to wait for the dawn.

The mysterious power of love integrates the many forces that now pull us apart; it brings us the wholeness that is our destiny. Love is not just a sentimental idea, and it is more than a good deed done. It is an attitude toward life and a pattern of living.

Love is not just something we feel; it is something we do. It is our abiding presence in the world.

Through us the power of love creates beautiful things to lift the spirit of the world. Through us the power of love soothes the wounds of those around us, mends the broken hearts, and gives them a sense of significance and belonging.

Through us the power of love opens the door to understanding, invites peace, and brings harmony in the midst of dissension. Love builds where hate destroys; it pacifies where aggression disturbs; it opens where pride closes.

Love does not make us weak. It does not ask us to surrender our personhood to the beloved, and it doesn't require self-abasement. Love is life-giving. It is a paradox: The more we give of it from our heart, the more our heart is filled with love, and the more we have to give.

Love inspires in us a special appreciation of ourselves and a respect for our own integrity. Love also takes us out of ourselves unto another. Through love we value another's uniqueness as a person.

To be peaceful we need not flee from our brothers and sisters in the world; rather, we must approach them through the heart, for through the heart all is made pure in the fire of love.

Love teaches us the significance of the other's individuality, while at the same time it reveals to us glimpses of our affiliation with all of humanity.

When we love, we stimulate the life-giving force within our brothers and sisters. We touch the source within them that activates their faith.

We must focus not on service but on loving. We let go and let our service overflow from our cup of love.

Love is not a passive attitude. It is a dynamic response to life. It is the enthusiasm of the soul.

We hear of love through the words of the poets, and we learn about love through the lives of saints and sinners. But we come to know love only by living it and by allowing it to be manifested as a true expression of our deepest nature.

Love is a reality that we must not deny. It is the foundation on which we must depend, the point on which we must focus. For the most part, the kind of love we offer to one another consists of a give-and-take between two persons. Consequently, when our relationship encounters a crisis of any kind, our love goes awry and begins to divide and destroy. Envy, jealousy, ambition, anger, and other hurtful passions run amok.

Love involves more than two persons; it is the concern of three — the lover, the beloved, and God, the source of all love.

When we love one another with God's love, we move from self-seeking to self-giving, from wanting to possess the one we love to working for his or her freedom.

When our love is motivated by the need to be exclusive, when it is based primarily on sensuality or self-interest, we are offering our own brand of love. When we love one another with God's love, we are carried outside of ourselves to a different dimension of love.

In giving to the person we love, the receiver also becomes a giver, and something beautiful is born of the union. To give life to something or someone through love is the greatest mutual experience two persons can have.

We are not called merely to love but to share in the divine love of God. To love one another, then, we must first be God-centered. God's penetration into our soul gives dynamic life to the love we offer to others.

To love we have to assemble the forces of our inner selves; in this way, loving brings us peace and integration. As we give to others of ourselves, we generate new life from within.

Only by loving, which is going beyond self unto another, can we hear the voice of God. Only by loving can his peace be ours. Love is the response of our souls to God. From love all life descends. To love all life ascends.

Keep yourselves in the love of God.

(Jude 1:21)

PAIN

Sometimes we find ourselves in a world of emotional pain with no relief in sight. We squirm in our anguish and beg for succor, but to no avail; for it seems the only way to the other side of the pain is to travel through its midst.

We hate pain and the misery of its wake. Some try to drown the pain with alcohol or numb it with other drugs. Sometimes we work ourselves into a state of fatigue in hope that we will be too worn out to feel the pain. We even try to pray the pain away. But any denial of the pain that comes only serves to intensify it and to compound our troubles. The truth is that pain cannot be avoided. It is a part of living and a part of loving.

Although pain affects all of us at one time or another, each of us chooses how we will respond to it; and therein lies the key that either opens our eyes to the benefit that may come from pain or imprisons us in perpetual fear and bitterness.

If we allow pain to overwhelm us, we are left vulnerable and in need of help from God and from our brothers and sisters. Pain reminds us that we are capable of being wounded and that we need healing. Having suffered the pain of life, we are more capable of compassion for the pain of others. Through our own pain, we acquire an empathy which we could acquire in no other way.

Pain may also teach us that the way we have been living is not effective for us, that we must change our ways or perish. It may reveal to us our true priorities. It may introduce us to our more sensitive and gentle side, the part of us that has been hidden under a hardened heart or a stubborn attitude.

We are called by love to be open to all that befalls us. It is in this receptive mode that we come to know the real joy of living. Here we deplete ourselves in order to be filled, we risk in order to be fully alive; and we dare to invest ourselves, even if we may be hurt.

When we accept pain as a part of life, we increase our capacity for endurance and we strengthen our ability to absorb the hurtful experiences that will come our way.

To "turn the other cheek" does not mean that we seek out pain. It means that once having been hurt by life, we keep on loving. We dare to love again, despite the pain inflicted.

We must be careful not to remain in pain for longer than is necessary. We are not to obsess in our pain. Rather, we need to allow it to run its course, remembering that it will not last forever. It will pass and leave its legacy of growth and maturity.

Of course, in the throes of our pain we cannot be expected to focus on the benefits that can come from our painful experiences. For now it is enough to stay with the pain when it comes. It is imperative that we not deny it or otherwise disrespect its presence. It will do its own work.

We need to receive all that life has to offer: ecstasy and joy, sorrow and pain. We should be willing to greet pain in all our vulnerability, not bracing against its impact, not disallowing its tempering effect. Waiting upon the Lord, we should let pain fulfill its purpose in us.

He will wipe every tear from their eyes, and there shall be no more death or mourning, wailing or pain, [for] the old order has passed away.

(Revelation 21:4)

PATIENCE

Patience is the midwife of peace. With her at our side, we give birth to serenity; without her, life is but a hurried, senseless journey through a barren land.

We scurry through life, full of desire to accomplish, only to discover that our race is in vain. And it takes us a long time to realize that the significance of any work correlates to the patience applied to it.

The quality of what we build and the beauty of what we create are at the mercy of our impatience. That which is lasting in structure and effect is that to which we have given the gift of patience.

We are easily distracted in our work by the demands for vast production and are tempted by the voices of greed that promise more for less. The result is craft without pride, literature without depth, labor without merit, and service without benefit.

Our patience, if we hold to it steadfastly, will help us to do the best we can with what we possess in time, textile, and talent. With patience the means become as important as the ends. When we set aside our own agenda to be really present to others, we exhibit one side of the triangle of patience.

Stopping to listen attentively to teenagers as they fantasize about their future — without ruining the moment with unnecessary reality — comes of patience. Taking the time to learn from and appreciate the reminiscences of the elderly comes of patience. Letting children develop at their own rate — especially in the academic field — without forcing them to meet some external standard of achievement, comes of patience.

The second side of the triangle concerns patience with ourselves.

We are easily disappointed when we do not meet the expectations we set for ourselves, although they usually tend to be perfectionistic and even a bit unrealistic. If we accept ourselves as we are and assess our possibilities and our limitations realistically, we are free to do what we can do and to be what we can be. Forgiving ourselves for our mistakes and not dwelling on our shortcomings release us from the jaws of our impatience and allow us to forge ahead with the business of living.

Sometimes the calamities that come our way push us to the brink of despair. We become tired of seeing our efforts produce little or no results, and we are greatly tempted to stop caring altogether. But patience with ourselves will help us see through another day.

The third side of the triangle has to do with God. We are told that our time is not God's time and our ways are not his; and yet we find ourselves drumming our fingers and tapping our feet, saying to God, "Hurry up. I don't have all day, you know."

So often we become anxious about the concerns of life and impatient about consequences which have nothing to do with us when — strained and tense — we wait nervously and impatiently. But this time can be used to restore the energy which we will be needing to deal with that for which we wait. By waiting on God we learn to live to the best of our abilities.

To be patient with God is to have faith, to be patient with ourselves is to have hope, and to be patient with others is to have love.

By your perseverance you will secure your lives.
(Luke 21:19)

PRAYER

Only prayer can free us of the thoughts and emotions which enslave our lives. Only prayer can open our hearts to the healing love of God.

But our prayer is like the desert rain; sometimes when we need it most, it doesn't come. No matter how desperate we become and how hard we try, our power to pray seems to disappear. We may manipulate our emotions through sweet music or compelling ritual, yet barren is the spirit. Eventually, we give up trying and let go of our control even over prayer. Then, like an illusive songbird, prayer seems to descend from nowhere and bursts into song.

We need to learn that prayer comes not at our initiative but God's. We discover that it takes much more than our emotions to pray, for prayer is an act of releasing our will to embrace his.

When we believe that prayer is something we do, we work overtime to communicate with God. But prayer is not something we do. It is something we allow to happen by being still and waiting for the God who comes. We are afraid to let go and begin a prayer which we do not control — because such prayer makes us more vulnerable than we want to be. It opens us to emotions and awareness that we are desperately trying to avoid. God's prayer in us is sometimes painful because as we enter into it we become conscious of the inordinate hold our selfish tendencies and false values have on us.

We fear the prayer of God in us because through it we discover just how poor we really are; it makes us acknowledge our powerlessness as human beings and our total dependence on God.

God's prayer in us does not necessarily include a sense of

religiosity, prayerfulness, or even faithfulness. It takes us as we are at a given moment. This reality is our prayer.

At first we may be moved to pray from our point of need, yet our prayer must move from mere petition to a union of love with God. God does intervene, but he does so less with the circumstances of our lives than with our manner of responding to those circumstances.

We should not seek to change our world through prayer; rather, we should let prayer change us as it changes our consciousness. We need to confront the God within, engage with him, and allow ourselves to be absorbed into his being.

In the midst of our prayerful selves we come to love God so much that we find ourselves surrendering our totality to him. This is the surrender that renders us free.

In prayer we yearn for the intimate presence of God and open ourselves to his life through us. Prayer is a power that flows through us when we submit to stillness of the soul. Only by daily communion with God will the spirit of peace descend upon us. It is the daily manna that brings us daily strength. And when we pray, the power of God is released into our world.

> **Pray that you have the strength to escape the tribulations that are imminent.**
>
> **(Luke 21:36)**

PRIORITIES

Choice is a double-edged sword. When we choose one direction, we must abandon another. Yet, in a life full of exciting options and varied interests, choices are hard to make.

Often we decide not to choose — thinking we can handle everything. We take on so much that we burn ourselves out. Instead of accomplishing all that we have taken on, we do nothing.

When we give in to the temptation of activism and overwork, when we comply with too many demands or volunteer for too many projects, we are heading for serious trouble. It is this overcommitment that is the source of much of our frustration, tension, and unwelcome stress.

Sometimes we take on too much because we are afraid to say "no." (But the real reason may be that we are afraid others will not approve of us if we decline.) At other times acceptance of overwork may come from overconfidence. We imagine we are like supermen and superwomen.

Some of us may be afraid of failure, so we set goals which are great and numerous. After all, no one can blame us if we fail to reach such grandiose goals. In effect we have programmed ourselves to fail. Sometimes we overload because we don't want to admit our limitations. We won't face the fact that we can't do it all. "If only we had a little more time," we say. But time is not the point at issue here; setting priorities for ourselves is. And to do that means making one choice over another.

For some of us it is difficult to realize that we are not responsible for everything. We are so busy meeting our own and others' expectations that we lose sight of what is really important.

"What are the top priorities in our lives?" "How important are they to us?" "Are we living our lives in accord with them?" "If not, what kind of choices should we make to reestablish their order of importance?" These are questions that we must ask ourselves.

Sometimes it takes a crisis in our lives to awaken us to what is really important for us. It may be a serious illness, a near-death, the death of a loved one, a divorce or alienation. Such catalysts are very painful, but we do not have to wait for a crisis before we get right with our priorities.

We need to ask ourselves some further — more soul-searching — questions. "Who am I?" "What do I have to work with?" "Where am I in life?" "How can this translate into the formation of priorities for me?"

We must look to our God-given abilities and talents. We must survey the circumstances of our lives, inventory our particular interests, and face the reality before us.

As we identify conflicting loyalties in our lives, we must have the courage to choose one and let go of the other. This conviction will surface for us as we focus in on our lives. From the quiet heart comes awareness of individual purpose in life. Our own singleness of purpose will give us a reference point from which all of our decisions will be made. Setting our priorities will lead to a simpler life.

Even after we have decided our priorities in life, we must revisit them periodically and check them out against the way we are living. We also need to allow for change in some of our priorities as we grow. Above all, we must constantly ask ourselves whether we are putting first in our lives that which we would give up last.

Where your treasure is, there also will your heart be.
(Matthew 6:21)

RESPECT
FOR
THE
BODY

We touch our spirituality not by the mortification of our body but by conscious respect for it.

In our attempt to control bodily passions and appetites, and because of preoccupation with mind games, we have become insensitive to our physical selves. Yet, our body is the first encounter we have with God. It is the most tangible manifestation of his love for us. It is the vehicle he uses to move in the world. Our body is the incarnation.

Of course, we become acutely aware of our body when we are sick or wounded. We know pain only too well, and our tendency is to avoid it whenever we can. But it is difficult to avoid pain because it is as a demanding child who screams for attention.

For the most part, we ignore our body until it is racked with pain and needs assistance. We also are ready to pay attention to our physical being as it appears to others: We work hard to trim our body, dress it up, gild it, shave it, manicure it, and otherwise make it attractive to others. What we do not do is become aware of our body for its own sake. We do not befriend it or take it with us as a moment-by-moment companion.

We are willing to acknowledge it when it hurts or malfunctions, but not when it operates normally and miraculously. We simply take it for granted and use it as we use a car or a bicycle. At the end of the day we park it very unceremoniously, only to start it up the next day. Our body is the vehicle of our mind (intellect) and our heart (emotion); it needs our time, our attention, and our respect.

Our mind can help our body to let go of its hold on fear and tension; and our body can, through this surrender, help our mind to venture into the realm of the spirit.

Slowly, slowly, our body breathes. There is a letting go of the tension in our head, a peace permeates our entire body, and our heart keeps the pace of life slow enough to appreciate God's presence within us.

Feel how the gravity of the earth pulls us into the chair in which we are sitting, urging us to let go, to be heavy and relaxed. Feel the bliss of muscles softening and clenched fists opening. Feel the life that comes to every tissue in our body as we breathe into our lungs, as our heart is nourished, as our blood travels to the farthest regions of our physical being to restore and heal and make whole.

Feel the death and resurrection as it happens to us cell by cell. Feel the warmth of our flesh and the texture of our skin. Feel the connectedness of all our physical members with one another and sense the unity of our bodies, our minds, and our emotions. Awareness of our body keeps us open to the full potential of our gifts. Awareness of our body keeps us centered on reality, for it is there that we discover our true being. Awareness of our body keeps us in the present, for it is only in the present that we can learn to love God.

Do you not know that you are the temple of God, and that the Spirit of God dwells in you?
(1 Corinthians 3:16)

REST

T hough we may live our life for God, we are not immune from physical, mental, and emotional exhaustion. We must constantly confront our limitations and discard the illusion that we are self-sufficient.

We are givers; yet first and foremost, we are receivers. Here lies the secret of a life of love: We must return to the source of all we are; we must take the time our soul requires in the quiet, in the still, in the real.

Letting go of the world and of all it demands of us brings rest to our soul. Our tired body relaxes more profoundly than even in sleep. Our mind dismisses the myriad of distractions that keeps it confused, and our emotions become more clear and more alive. This integration of the spirit allows the abundant life that is our inheritance.

The time we need to be alone and be nourished in the arms of God will not likely be found in the ordinary course of daily life. Like a long-lost treasure it must be sought. Once found, we must guard it jealously against those who would steal it from us, leaving us to die of spiritual starvation.

Sometimes it is those who love us the most who do not understand our need to be absent from them and present to ourselves and to our God. Yet, it is for them as much as for ourselves that we must leave the crowd, not to return until our wholeness has been restored.

Our time away may not always be extensive. Sometimes we may be able to carve only minutes of repose out of our entire day. This will be sufficient if, during the brief escape, we focus on the spirit within. It is this focus that brings about our integration, if only for a while. Small segments of time for ourselves will be enough for our spiritual health if they are frequent and consistent. Our time-outs must become as regular a part of living as sitting down for a meal.

The new life that comes from taking the time to prune that which is not of God carries with it its own danger. Even in our wholeness we are apt to quickly forget that we are but the branches, completely dependent upon the vine. When we remember that we can move only because we have stopped, that we can work only because we have rested, that we can give only because we have received, and that we can love only because we have been loved, then we will go again into the hills to pray.

> **Whoever enters into God's rest, rests from his own works as God did from his.**
>
> **(Hebrews 4:10)**

SELF-ESTEEM

In the name of humility we often deny ourselves one of the most basic of human needs: our self-esteem (self-worth). He may *think* we are unworthy of glory; but the fact is that without self-esteem, we wither and die psychologically and spiritually.

Not how others see us, but who we are is the point of issue. We are children of God, created in his image. The unconditional love we have for ourselves is not earned; it is given to us by God.

When we feel estranged from God, we usually feel low self-esteem. If we cut ourselves off from the source of self-love, we lose our self-esteem.

To enhance our self-esteem we must reject any teaching that would have us demean or destroy the ego. Instead, we need to follow the path that redeems it as the presence of God on earth.

Often we decry self-esteem because we equate it with conceit. But self-esteem is pride in being a human being. Conceit is the result of comparing ourselves with others and allocating to ourselves an unwarranted high regard.

True self-esteem indicates our awareness and appreciation of God's work within us.

Rejoice...your reward will be great in heaven.
(Matthew 5:12)

SHALOM

Shalom! May the peace of love embrace you and carry you through the storms of life!

This is not the peace the world offers. It comes from the fountain of our own hearts. It is a consequence of our daily living. It blossoms in the midst of order — that tranquility of mind that prevails when our true priorities are established and followed.

Peace would be ours if only we would let go of our preoccupation with ourselves. Until we see ourselves as we really are and accept ourselves as such, we will not experience peace. It comes to us when we place our hope beyond ourselves. It will be ours when we acknowledge that we are nothing but souls absorbed in loving attention to the One from whom we come.

The absence of anxiety and fear is not peace, nor is an easy and harmless life an indication of peace. Peace can be ours even in the midst of trouble. Peace is a knowledge in the depth of our souls that we are not alone. The eternal is with us always.

Peace comes only within the framework of the present moment. It manifests itself when we let go of yesterday and let tomorrow take care of itself.

We will be distracted, by the ways of the world, but we must not despair. We are rooted in the soil of love. If we focus on love, we will have peace.

Peace be with you.

(3 John 1:15)

SIMPLICITY

S implicity is the fruit of focalized living.

Most of us fill our days with the anxiety of duplicity. We allow the media to tell us what we need; we listen to others tell us how we should be, becoming confused by all the choices that are offered; we attempt to accumulate money and possessions, as if more was necessarily better; and we are divided unto ourselves by a myriad of gods who attract us and then enslave us.

"Simplify, simplify," counsels Thoreau; yet this is easier said than done. How are we to be simple in a world that is becoming more complex by the minute? How are we to simplify when our state in life demands so much from us?

How can we simplify our lives? Must we sell our possessions, quit our jobs, go off into the desert? Need we grow our own food, refuse to accept the latest style changes, stop learning new information?

No. External action on our part will not result in simplicity. No particular lifestyle will ensure it. It is a state of mind, the consequence of how we live our moments internally. But if we pursue it for its own sake, it becomes just another object of our ambition; and in our pursuit of it, we chase it away.

Simplicity comes from a word meaning single, or one. Yet our life is, for the most part, riddled with duplicity. We disrupt our living by having too many irons in the fire, by not deciding what is the most important thing for us and living accordingly.

In every case of conflict or complication we are apt to discover that we either do not know what is best for us or we confuse the secondary with the primary. We bind ourselves to duplicity when we fail to choose from among the competing attachments the one which we should hold above all others.

If we focus inwardly on the "one thing necessary," we free ourselves from the chains of anxiety, bringing peace and unity to our external living. This internal focus on the kingdom of God calls us to a radical obedience to the Sovereign of our life. We obey God in his laws of nature, whether physical or psychological. We obey God when we hold him hallowed above all else and love him with all our being.

Our internal focus on the kingdom of God reveals our total dependence on God. We depend on him for the very faith that causes us to believe in him. We depend on God for our daily bread, which nourishes us through the physical, emotional, and psychological famines of our lives. We depend on him for the living water that sustains us through the drought of the soul. There is nothing more important than to hunger and thirst for communion with God.

The renouncement of the external, whether it be wealth, the opinion of others, or addictions, does not bring us simplicity; but our surrender to the kingdom of God detaches us from all the rest to the extent that we can put it into perspective and manage it effectively in our lives.

The internal focus on the kingdom of God affects the way we think, feel, and act. It singularly affects the decisions we make about possessions, relationships, and lifestyles. We become simple from the inside out.

We will always be anxious about not getting what we need. We will need security, love, and order in our lives; and to secure them we need simplicity.

Seek first the kingdom [of God]...and all these things will be given you besides.

(Matthew 6:33)

SUFFERING

S uffering is an integral part of living. It is the thread that weaves fineness into the fabric of humanity. Love of God is the thread that gives it strength and durability.

When we encounter suffering in our daily lives, we try to flee from it by numbing ourselves. We ignore the question of the meaning of our suffering by getting lost in the crowd or by riding a merry-go-round that goes nowhere. We seek rest from suffering through stupefying distractions and the deceptive peace of drugs.

We want the power to control the suffering that comes. We want to believe in something or someone who can show us the path away from suffering, but we will not escape our suffering. In fact, the seed of hope is in this apparent hopelessness. In our weakness there is strength; in our brokenness, wholeness; and in our powerlessness there is the potential for transformation.

Yet, from the suffering we face can come our transformation. By loving God with a purity of heart and the intensity of fire, we conquer the temptation of despair.

As we embrace our suffering, we come to know the feelings of sadness, dejection, grief, loneliness, fear, discouragement, weariness, terror, physical agony, and even spiritual abandonment. Yet, as human beings we remain distinguishable from the circumstances of our lives. Our identity is not in what happens to us but in how we respond to it.

Victor Frankl went through hell on earth as a prisoner of the Dachau and Auschwitz concentration camps, yet all the while he preserved his personal integrity.

He believed that although human beings are not free from those conditions which are imposed by life or by others, be they physical, psychological, or sociological, they always remain free to take a stand toward these conditions. Frankl was convinced that human beings always retain the freedom to choose their attitude toward life.

Frankl used his sense of humor as well as daily goal-setting for himself just to stay alive in the concentration camps. Of course, he acquiesced to the demands of the guards, just as we must do to those who hold power and authority over us. But he never let them enter the sanctuary of his soul. There he took his last stand. There he concentrated all his force.

Frankl held that by taking a stand toward suffering and giving it meaning and purpose, human beings transcend the world and the predicament in which they are caught.

Upon entering Auschwitz, Frankl was forced to give up his clothes and put on those of a man who had already been sent to the gas chamber. In the pocket of the man's clothes Frankl found a single page torn from a Hebrew prayer book. On it were the words of the traditional Jewish prayer: "Love thy God with all thy heart, and with all thy soul, and with all thy might." Frankl interpreted this as a command to say "yes" to life no matter what a person faces, including suffering or even death.

This is not a Pollyanna approach to life in which we see our suffering through rose-colored glasses. These are the choices we make every day, choices about how we will respond to what life brings with it.

The morning paper tells of a mother whose fifteen-year-old daughter was burned to the bone on her arms, neck, and face by a would-be rapist who poured a caustic chemical on her. Imagine the feelings of a mother in such circumstances. Certainly despair and surrender to death would be great temptations; yet the mother chose otherwise. Her disfigured teenager would "rise like the Phoenix and hold her own in society," she said.

This is not a denial of evident misery but a decision on how she will respond to that misery and what she will carve out of the tragic circumstances.

She has had to let go of the dreams she had for her daughter. She has had to let go of life as she would have preferred it; yet she has not let go of that indestructible being within from which comes solace, hope, and purpose to go on living.

For as Christ's sufferings overflow to us, so through Christ does our encouragement also overflow.
(2 Corinthians 1:5)

SURRENDERING THE HEART

In the desert of life we reach the point of full surrender. Here in our poverty of soul we release our hold on the ephemeral and embrace the eternal.

We, who have turned to God to meet our basic needs, discover that he offers so much more than this. Beyond our satisfaction, we are nourished by God's gifts of love and mercy. From his bounty we receive the treasures of the heart which will not be taken from us.

"One does not live by bread alone, but by every word that comes forth from the mouth of God" (Matthew 4:4). These words of God are spoken in our hearts. He tells us of his love for us and of his will. Only when we set aside our preoccupation with the satisfaction of our needs will we hear his voice.

In our surrender into the arms of God we are no longer concerned for our hunger and thirst except as they lead us closer to him. His words of intimacy and communion nourish us beyond our expectations.

We, who have looked to God to protect us from all harm, come to discover that he offers so much more. It is his will that we be safe and sound, but more than that, he would save our souls.

In our fear of the world around us we neglect the care of the world within us. In the name of faith we cast God in the role of great protector, while at the same time we continue to live our lives according to our will. But we are warned: "You shall not put the Lord, your God, to the test" (Matthew 4:7).

In our surrender to the care of God we get more than security. We enter into our vulnerability and transcend pain, suffering, and even death as we carry our cross with the strength of God. We will not escape the harm of a cruel and dangerous world, but we will respond to it with the power of God's merciful love.

In our zeal to serve the world we get caught up in the process and forget about the Source of all loving service. We become so busy and involved with our work, our church, our community, and our family that we forget to return to God in prayer and contemplation.

Sometimes the gods we choose to worship in our lives become so paramount that they take us away from the God who offers so much more. We may become worshipers and servers of our work, our addictions, our drugs, our obsessions and compulsions, our money, our possessions, our power, and other all-absorbing preoccupations. But we are admonished: "The Lord, your God, shall you worship and him alone shall you serve" (Matthew 4:10).

When we surrender to God, we are freed from the imprisonment of our false gods. Turning wholly and unconditionally to God and worshiping him as our one and only God, we become integrated and spiritually healthy once again.

Our surrender to God does not happen once and for all. It is a process by which we run gently, but firmly, as we return to where we belong.

> **Remember the days past when, after you had been enlightened, you endured a great contest of suffering.**
>
> **(Hebrews 10:32)**

TAKING TIME

Sometimes life seems to be more than we can handle. We may be overwhelmed by the huge task before us, or we may be crushed by the giant expectations of the future. We say, "This is too much for me," and we become immobilized.

It may be that we are facing a life without the presence of a loved one because of death, divorce, or separation. It may be a permanent physical disability that confronts us or a job so big and complicated that it appears impossible to do. It may be a myriad of problems coming at us from all directions that has us feeling overpowered. Whatever the case, the common denominator is that it is too much to do or to bear all at once. It seems beyond our capacity at the moment. Our temptation, then, is to allow the circumstances of life to overwhelm us, swallow us up, and defeat us, even before we begin.

It is easy to become discouraged when we consider the whole job that needs to be done. No wonder we become depressed when we look at an entire life of difficulty. Of course, we despair when we stand before the mountain that needs to be moved with nothing but our little shovel.

What we are capable of at a given moment is no match for the whole of what confronts us. But therein lies the problem. When we compare our moment — which is all we really have — with a week, a month, a year, or a lifetime; or when we compare what we are capable of doing now with the completion of a giant task before us;

or when we compare the intensity of the grief we feel this moment with the prospect of feeling this way forever, then, of course, we are vanquished.

It is only when we become more realistic that we can cope with the life before us. The reality is that we don't have to live our whole lives in one moment, we don't have to experience all the grief of a lifetime right now, and we don't have to accomplish the big job all at once. We can take our time.

We should focus on what we can do now, what we can experience now, what we can realistically expect from ourselves now. We cannot expand ourselves through our anxiety. Rather, our task is to take what is before us and break it down into bite-size portions which we can chew and swallow without choking.

It is within our capacity to suffer a tragedy one moment at a time. We can realize a grand goal eventually by taking time to achieve one objective toward that goal in the moment at hand. We can move the mountain by concentrating on one shovelful at a time.

Breaking down a workweek, a complicated task, or a troubled time of life into what is manageable for us requires humble recognition of our limitations. In segments we can handle a given situation, we can bear it, we can accomplish it.

When we are overwhelmed with life, it is usually because we are trying to live it all at once. We must come to believe that God gives us all that we need to handle what is before us now — if we take our time.

Do not worry about tomorrow; tomorrow will take care of itself. Sufficient for a day is its own evil.

(Matthew 6:34)

TEARS

Tears are signs of life that rise from the wellspring of the soul. Tears are gifts from God that cleanse and salve our wounded hearts. Tears are real. Tears are revealing. Tears are the commonality between every man and every woman.

No matter how calloused we've become through the barrage of suffering and violence in our world, the misfortune of one single person may move us to shed the tears of compassion.

Sometimes the joy that overwhelms us, even for a moment, taps that reservoir of emotion that lies in our depths, and the tears will come.

The profound sorrow that overcomes us in an hour of loneliness, despair, or grief brings with it the tears of life that moisten even the driest of deserts.

Our tears of sadness actually release a toxic element from our system; but more importantly, they release the tension that builds within us. Tears release us from the prison of apathy and carry us into the freedom of human emotion.

It may be the sight of a young father looking with adoration at his newborn child that brings a tear to our eyes. It may be the realization that our "baby" is now grown up, or it may be the pain of loss on viewing our changing world that prompts our tears. It may even be a brief second in the midst of our prayer into which we enter the ecstasy of our divinity that we shed the tears of our humanity.

Even when we don't want to cry, we cry, because tears will not be controlled. They remain for us the true gauge of our emotions and do not countenance manipulation.

Tears are part of our spontaneity, and as such they come and go according to the experiences of our hearts. To hold back a tear that must be shed is to dam the river of life. To let it flow is to acknowledge and allow our total selves.

Tears surprise us sometimes because they seem to know more about our true feelings than we do. When we least expect it, they let us know that something we've been minimizing is actually very important to us, or that something hurts us much more than we are willing to admit.

Tears emanate from the strength of spirit that dares to be vulnerable. Tears are not a sign of weakness; rather, they are a manifestation of the courage it takes to be fully human and fully alive.

I have heard your prayer and seen your tears. I will heal you.

(2 Kings 20:5)

VULNERABILITY

Love goes beyond giving to receiving. As lovers, we are to nurture our beloved; and as the beloved, we are to relax and relish the nurturing that is given to us.

Some of us refuse to be on the receiving end of nurturing because we are afraid that we will lose control of the situation if we change from giver to receiver. As long as we can remain in control and can decide just how involved to become with others, we are all right. Otherwise, we panic.

Some of us are fearful of being nurtured by others because this leaves us vulnerable. Exposing ourselves to nurturing is risky business. When we are wounded by others, it is better, we think, to go without the nurturing we so desperately need than to risk being hurt.

Others of us turn down nurturing because we are afraid we may like it and even become dependent on it. If we don't get any, we won't miss it; but if we get some, we may want to keep getting it. We fear that would mean the end of our self-sufficiency.

Fear keeps us trembling alone beneath the suit of armor we wear for the world. It is fear of being judged by others that has us wearing a mask of our partial selves. It is fear of being controlled or hurt by those who know wherein lies our "Achilles heel" that prompts us to encrust ourselves inside protective shells.

We may be protected against discovery; but, at the same time, we are cut off from the help, the nurturing, and the love others want to give us.

Pride also plays a part in our charade. When we pretend to be more than we are by hiding our vulnerability from others, we are telling them that we don't need what they have to give. We are deciding that we are self-sufficient, islands unto ourselves. But, in truth, we are not self-sufficient. We need to be intimate with others, and we cannot be intimate without first becoming vulnerable.

Being vulnerable means that we are willing to expose all of our sides, even when we may be hurt by doing so. It doesn't mean we must open ourselves, all the time, to everybody. Self-preservation requires that we pick carefully the one to whom we show our vulnerability. But in the final analysis, vulnerability is based not on trust but risk. This is why it is so scary.

What happens when we dare to be vulnerable with others? What happens when others see our weaknesses as well as our strengths; our liabilities as well as our assets; our ugliness as well as our beauty; our humanness as well as our divinity?

What happens is that we give other persons an opportunity to get to know the real us, to embrace the whole us. We give them the opportunity to be strong for us, to complement our deficiencies with their gifts, and above all, to accept us as we truly are.

When others accept, love, and even like us, after we have exposed our vulnerabilities to them, we no longer have to wonder, "Would they love me if they knew all of me?" We can relax and know we are loved, not for our facades but for our total selves.

It is a risk to be vulnerable because we may, in fact, be hurt. Here is where we turn the other cheek. Here is where we love enough to stay. Here is where we risk again.

One meaning of the word *vulnerable* is "to be capable of being wounded." It also means to be capable of loving and being loved.

But what anyone dares to boast of...I also dare.
(2 Corinthians 11:21)

WHOLENESS

Our wholeness depends on balancing our spiritual selves with our physical and mental selves. Each gives to the other. The denial or exaggeration of one brings death to all three of them.

We need to become conscious of who we are: We are of this earth. Here we live and bear our fruit, but we must never forget that our origins are in heaven. We must constantly acknowledge our finite being and, at the same time, remember that we have an infinite source and destiny.

Our task in life is to resist anything that threatens wholeness, whether it be lust, anger, worry, or an unbridled intellectualism.

The obstacles to our wholeness lie not outside of us but within us. We think too much. We look too much into the future, and this brings about unnecessary fear. We are not tranquil as is the rest of nature. Nature rests in what it is without thinking what it wishes to become. The pull between what we are and what we wish to become is a tension which keeps us disintegrated.

Another tension that breaks the harmony of life is our fear of death with which we are so preoccupied. In our effort to escape death, we waste precious living time.

We are one with the universe, yet we break that union by believing ourselves to be separate and absolute. We end up lonely and isolated. We are lost because of our fear of becoming involved, our fear of becoming vulnerable, and our fear of losing ourselves.

Our religion is our salvation. A candle cannot burn without a fire, and man cannot live without a spiritual life. But religion is not just a notion about God. Rather, it is a transforming experience. It is a matter of personal realization. Creeds and dogmas, words and symbols, are merely instruments through which our religion is expressed.

Spirituality has to do with becoming free and breaking the chains of convention. It shuns the multitude of opinions which are offered in the name of religion.

The name by which we choose to call God is not as important as the way we come to him. What matters is that in single-minded sincerity we seek union with the divine life.

In our journey toward wholeness we are not asked to lose ourselves but to discover our truest selves at our deepest level. Spiritual persons are not those who just go off by themselves to pray but those who also seek union with the divine life in the midst of daily living.

Spirituality is not an escape from our responsibilities in life; it is not a fantasy with which we play. We can attain our immortal destiny here and now. As we work in the world, we become channels for the divine influence.

> **Whoever finds his life will lose it, and whoever loses his life for my sake will find it.**
>
> **(Matthew 10:39)**